contents

editor's note

The Irish Theatre Handbook illustrates the current strength and vitality of the professional drama and dance scene in Ireland.   Its arrival further emphasises the incredible growth in the sector and attempts to put a shape on what is now a hugely complex and interconnected industry.   Fifty-four subsidised companies and fifty-three non-subsidised companies are listed, along with forty-four programming venues and thirteen festivals, giving some idea of the power and voraciousness of the creative beast that now runs alongside the Celtic Tiger.

The Handbook is an initiative of the Theatre Shop (an organisation that addresses and promotes Irish theatre in an international context).   Its primary purpose therefore, is to promote the work of Irish companies both at home and abroad.   It is hoped that the Handbook would also serve as an invaluable resource guide for the entire industry and as a means of disseminating information on all aspects of the sector in an organised and comprehensive manner.

A very significant feature of the Handbook is the three appendices which detail every single new Irish play, dance work and opera produced over the past ten years by the current subsidised sector. The New Irish Plays appendix is included to counteract the severe paucity of Irish playscripts currently being published.   It is hoped that the appendix will serve as a statement of a body of work while simultaneously reintroducing many neglected plays into the repertoire.   The appendix of new Irish Dance Works is included for similar reasons, but also to enhance the ongoing debate regarding the choreographers right to claim 'authorship' of their work and be regarded as 'creative' as opposed to 'interpretative' artists.

The editorial guidelines exercised in compiling the directory was as follow:

* Subsidised companies were defined as those in receipt of 'revenue' or 'project' funding from The Arts Council/An Chomhairle Ealaíon or 'revenue' funding from the Arts Council of Northern Ireland.

* Nonsubsidised companies were defined as all other professional theatre and dance companies based in the Republic of Ireland and Northern Ireland.

* The venues and festivals listed are those which are professionally managed and actively programming a significant quantity of professional theatre and dance productions on an ongoing basis.

It is hoped that the Irish Theatre Handbook will continue to develop as an annual publication. Companies or individuals interested in being included in future publications are invited to submit information to The Theatre Shop for consideration.

Loughlin Deegan	Ciara McGlynn	Martin Munroe	Siobhan Bourke
Editor	Administrator	Co-ordinator	Producer

A note on phone numbers: In listing telephone and fax numbers in the Irish Theatre Handbook we have included local area codes only.   The relevant direct dialling international codes are as follows:
Republic of Ireland: 00 353.   **Great Britain** *(including Northern Ireland for callers outside the Republic):* 00 44
Northern Ireland *(for callers from the Republic):* 08

subsidised companies

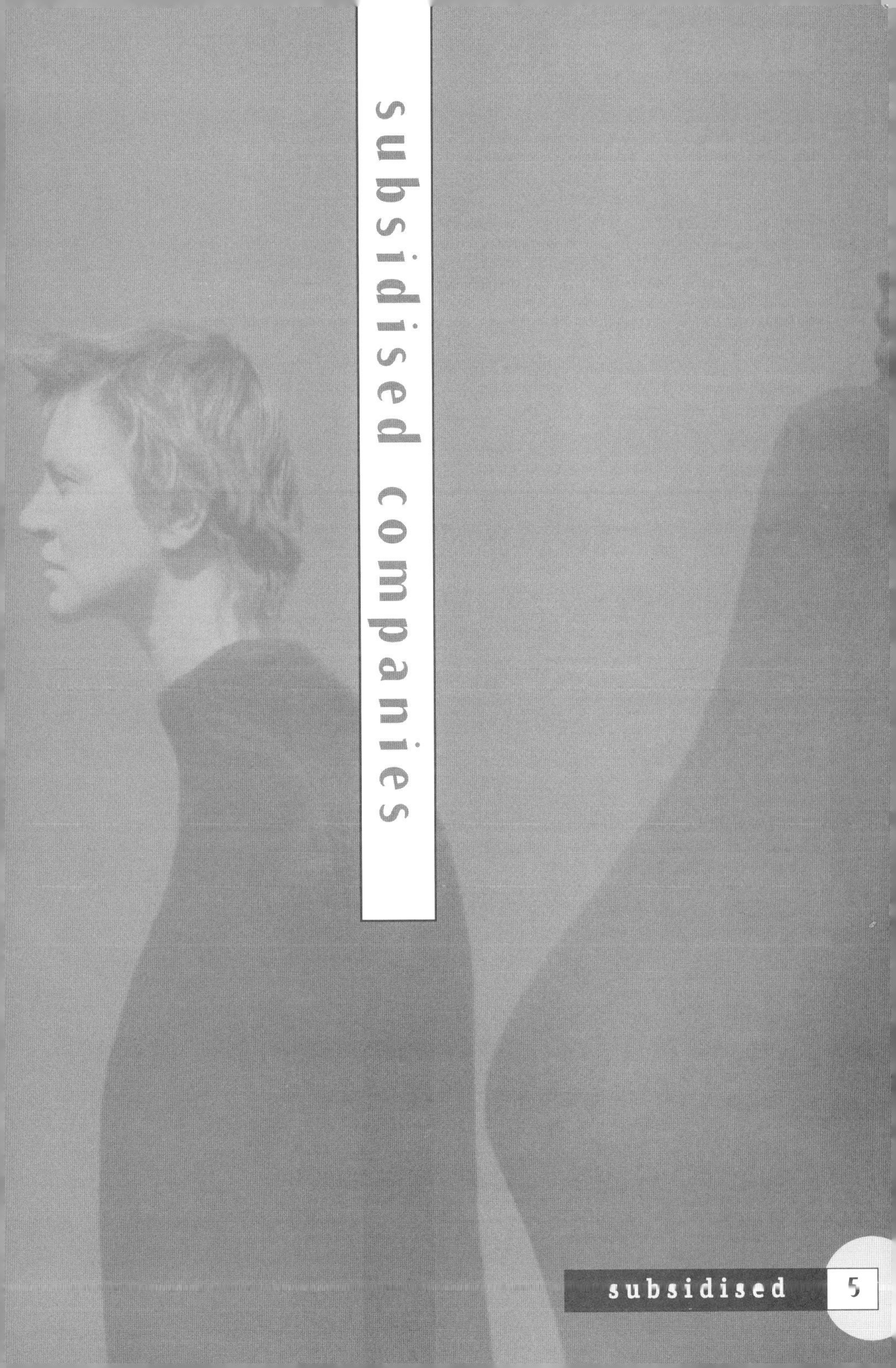

Aisling Ghéar's artistic policy is to consolidate and develop Irish language theatre in Belfast and throughout Ireland on a professional basis and to establish and promote the highest standards in all aspects of Irish language theatre including playwriting, acting and directing.

Aisling Ghéar

12 Cearnóg An Choláiste Thuaidh
Béal Feirste BT1 6AS
Tel: 01232 331131
Fax: 01232 331132

Admin contact: Róisín Ní Sheanáin,
Máire Andrews
Artistic contact: Gearóid Ó Cairealláin

Officially launched in September 1997, Aisling Ghéar is the north's first professional Irish language theatre company. The company evolved from Belfast based amateur group Aisteoirí Aon Dráma. The name Aisling Ghéar means Sharp Vision.

Recent Productions:
'Liacreidimh' - a bilingual production of 'Faith Healer' by Brian Friel.
'Bás Taismeach Ainrialaí' - a translation of 'Accidental Death of an Anarchist' by Dario Fo.
'Republica' by Aodh Ó Dhomhnaill.

Recent Touring, Ireland:
'Lia Creidimh'.
'Bás Taismeach Ainrialaí'.

Photo: Scene from 'Accidental Death of an Anarchist'.
© Phil Smyth.

Amharclann de hÍde

Upper Courtyard
Dublin Castle
Dublin 2
Tel: 01 4754901
Fax: 01 4754898
E-mail: adehide@indigo.ie

Admin contact: Emíl Ní Chuilinn
Artistic contact: Bríd Ó Gallchóir

Amharclann de hÍde, in its sixth year, embarked on a number of new projects: the development of writing groups in the Gaeltacht areas; workshopping and, for the first time, devising new work with writers such as Alan Titley and Liam Ó Muirthile. In 1999, the company is looking forward to its first international tour, when it will tour to America and Canada with Liam Ó Muirthile's 'Tine Chnámh', a revival of the company's first production.

The award winning company was founded in 1992 with the aim of commissioning new work in the Irish language and, through the use of the language, to create a distinct aesthetic and a vibrant, alternative form of theatre.

Recent Productions:
'Milseog an tSamhraidh' (1997 Dublin Theatre Festival, Beckett Centre).
'Buile an Phíce' (1997, Andrews Lane, Dublin).
'Chun na Farraige Síos', 'Pósadh an Tincéra' (1996, Scoil Náthaigh).
'Fear an Tae' (1995, Andrews Lane, Dublin).

Recent Touring, Ireland:
'Chun na Farraige Síos', 'Pósadh an Tincéra' (1996, extensive tour of Gaeltacht areas, Derry and Belfast).

Photo: (Left to Right) Brian Thunder,
Liam Heffernan, Mary Ryan, Diarmaid de Faoite and Cathy
Belton in 'Tine Chnámh'
© Liam Ó Muirthile.

The Ark - A Cultural Centre For Children

Eustace Street
Temple Bar
Dublin 2
Tel: 01 6707788
Fax: 01 6707758
E-mail: info@ark.ie
Website: http://www.ark.ie

Admin contact: Phill McCaughey
Artistic contact: Martin Drury

The Ark is an arts centre dedicated to producing high-quality work across the arts for children aged 3 - 13 years. Ten programmes are produced annually, many involving work commissioned from artists of all disciplines.

Recent Productions:
'The Dream Factory' (1998).
'The Pied Piper' (1998).
'The Christmas Café' (1997).

Photo: Colin O'Neill and Orlando Schenk in
'The Pied Piper' by Johnny Hanrahan and
John Browne. © Tommy Clancy.

Barabbas are dedicated to dynamic and physical theatre, theatre with roots in the European continent but that has gone on to explore Irish gesture, Irish aural and visual culture.

Barabbas...
the company Ltd.

7 South Great Georges Street
Dublin 2
Tel: 01 6712013
Fax: 01 6704275
E-mail: barabbas@indigo.ie

Admin contact: Enid Reid Whyte,
Company Manager.
Artistic contact: Veronica Coburn,
Artistic Director.

Barabbas, one of Ireland's most successful physical theatre companies was founded in 1993 by Veronica Coburn, Raymond Keane and Mikel Murfi. The company's work includes theatre, television and training. Based in Dublin, the company has toured in Ireland and abroad.

Recent Productions:
'The Whiteheaded Boy' by Lennox Robinson (1997-98).
'Out The Back Door' by Barabbas...the company (1997) - see also The Ark.
'Strokehauling' by Barabbas...the company (1996-97).
'Half Eight Mass Of A Tuesday' by Barabbas...the company (1996).

Recent Touring, Ireland
'The Whiteheaded Boy', 1998.
'Strokehauling', 1997.
'Macbeth', 1995.

Recent Touring, Overseas
'The Whiteheaded Boy' (1998).
'Strokehauling' (1997).
'Half Eight Mass of A Tuesday' (1996).

Photo: (Left to Right) Mikel Murphi,
Veronica Coburn and Raymond Keane in
'The Whiteheaded Boy'. © Levin McFeely.

Barnstorm - Kilkenny Theatre Arts

Good Sheperd Centre
Church Lane, Kilkenny
Tel: 056 51266 / 70495
Fax: 056 51266
E-mail: barnstorm@tinet.ie

Admin contact: Vincent Dempsey,
General Manager.
Artistic contact: Philip Hardy,
Artistic Director.

Established in 1991 Barnstorm's work is now divided into five categories: Theatre For Young Audiences - presenting high quality, professional theatre to young people which speaks directly to its audience; Youth Theatre - serves young people 10 - 25 years in age in Kilkenny through weekly drama workshops, and the development and presentation of plays; Outreach Programmes - facilitates a variety of theatre/drama projects in the community; Community Theatre Projects - working with an entire community to research, devise and present theatre which is reflective of their own lives and experiences; New Writing - collaborating with various writers the company seeks to develop forms of theatre and new styles of performance which will engage the range of audiences it serves.

Recent Productions:
'Silly Bits of Sky' by Maeve Ingoldsby.
'When Moses Met Marconi' by Bernard Farrell.
'The Comer Story' by Ken Bourke.
'Bananas In The Bread Bin' by Maeve Ingoldsby.

Recent Touring, Ireland:
'Silly Bits of Sky' by Maeve Ingoldsby.
'When Moses Met Marconi' by Bernard Farrell.
'Bananas In The Bread Bin' by Maeve Ingoldsby.

Photo: William O'Connell and Michael Carberry in 'Silly Bits Of Sky'. ©Ciaran O'Keefe.

Bedrock

36/37 Lower Ormond Quay
Dublin 1
Tel: 01 8729300
Fax: 01 8729478
E-mail: bedrock@clubi.ie

Admin contact: Irene Kernan
Artistic contact: Jimmy Fay

Bedrock was established in 1993. The company produces works by new and established writers from Ireland and the rest of Europe. In 1995, Bedrock initiated and administered the Dublin Fringe Festival.

Bedrock looks beyond the accepted canon of Irish and International drama to produce work which participates in the changes and conflicts of modern life and which upsets established certainties of what theatre is for and how it should be done.

Recent Productions:
'Deep Space' by Alex Johnston.
'Greek' by Steven Berkoff.
'Quartet' by Heiner Müller.
'Electroshock - A Theatre of Cruelty Season.'

Recent Touring, Ireland:
'Greek' - Belltable Arts Centre, Limerick.

Recent Touring, Overseas:
'Deep Space' (1998, Adelaide Fringe Festival, Australia & The Bush Theatre, London).

Photo: (Left to Right) Alex Johnston as Keith and Patrick Leech as Jaco in 'Deep Space' by Alex Johnston.
© Vincent O'Byrne.

Belfast Theatre Company

207 Russell Court
Claremont Street
Belfast BT9 6JX
Tel: 01232 596814
Fax: 01232 596814

Contact: Paddy Scully

Belfast Theatre Company is a professional company financed in part by the Arts Council of Northern Ireland and Belfast City Council. The company's performances are designed for touring across Ireland and further afield. The company was a winner of a BBC New Drama Award in 1995/6 and was nominated for several Irish Times and other drama awards. It also won a Pick of the Fringe in Edinburgh 1983 with 'Shem the Penman'.

The company's artistic policy is to promote new and innovative drama, especially from Northern Ireland.

Recent Productions:
'The Feast of Lupercal' (1997).
'The Family Album of J. Edgar Hoover' (1996).
'A Most Notorious Woman' (1997/98)

Recent Touring, Ireland:
'The Feast of Lupercal' (1997).
'A Most Notorious Woman' (1997/98).

Recent Touring, Overseas:
'The Family Album of J.Edgar Hoover' (U.K. and Europe).
'Shem the Penman' (U.K. and Europe).

Photo: Toby Byrne and Laura Hughes in 'The Feast of Lupercal'. © Brian Thompson Photography.

Bickerstaffe Theatre Company

50 John Street
Kilkenny
Tel: 056 51254
Fax: 056 63679

Admin contact: Lynn Cahill,
Richard Cook

Bickerstaffe Theatre Company produces new Irish plays by commission. Also produces an annual open-air Shakespeare production and the highly successful Cat Laughs comedy festival.

Recent Productions:
'Much Ado About Nothing' by William Shakespeare.
Cat Laughs Festival.
'Easter Dues' by John Waters.
'Hard to Believe' by Conall Morrison.

Recent Touring, Ireland:
'Hard To Believe'.
'Double Helix'.
'True Lines'.

Recent Touring, Overseas:
'True Lines' toured to the Bush Theatre, London.

Photo: Ronan Wilmot and Owen O'Neil in Bickerstaffe's production of 'Much Ado About Nothing' at Kilkenny Castle, August 1998. © Dylan Vaughan.

Big Telly creates dynamic and visual theatre. The company produces theatre incorporating music and rhythm, movement and dance, masks, puppet making and circus skills to invigorate and challenge the presentation of our work.

Recent Productions:
'To Hell With Faust' (1998, co-production with the Lyric Players Theatre, Belfast).
'Metamorphosis' (1996, in association with the Riverside Theatre, Coleraine).
'Wild Child' (1996).
'Cuchulainn' (1995, in association with the Riverside Theatre, Coleraine).

Big Telly Theatre Company Ltd.

Portstewart Town Hall
The Crescent
Portstewart BT55 7AB
Tel: 01265 832588
Fax: 01265 832588
E-mail: bigtelly@dnet.co.uk
Website: www.artspark.net/home/bigtelly

Recent Touring, Ireland:
'To Hell With Faust' - National tour (1998).
'Metamorphosis' - National tour (1996).
'Wild Child' - Tour of schools in Northern Ireland (1996).

Admin contact: Úna E. Kealy / Bernie McGill
Artistic contact: Zoë Seaton

Photo: Paula McFetridge and Richard Croxford in 'To Hell With Faust'. © Seamus Loughrey.

Big Telly produces original scripts by company members and existing texts. The company tours on average one major production per year, as well as investing in community and education projects closer to home.

Blue Raincoat Theatre Company

The Blue Raincoat Theatre Company
'The Factory Performance Space'
Lower Quay Street
Sligo
Tel: 071 70431
Fax: 071 70431
E-mail: bluerain@iol.ie
Admin contact: Rory Concannon
Artistic contact: Niall Henry

Blue Raincoat Theatre Company is a professional theatre company based in Sligo. The Company was founded in 1991. Since its foundation Blue Raincoat have staged 27 professional productions. Full clients of The Arts Council of Ireland, Blue Raincoat Theatre Company owns and operates its own 160 seat performance venue, The Factory Performance Space in central Sligo, and also operates extensive public research facilities.

For seven years, Blue Raincoat Theatre Company have cultivated a growing national audience and the highest of theatrical reputations through work staged for the most part at their home in Sligo. Last year saw Blue Raincoat Theatre Company touring their highly acclaimed production of 'A Midsummer Night's Dream' which visited Sligo, Galway, Cork, Waterford, Dublin and London. This year Blue Raincoat plan to tour their latest Shakespearean production 'The Tempest' to venues in the North of Ireland to continue its policy of audience development throughout Ireland.

Recent Productions:
'The Tempest' by William Shakespeare (January 1998)
'A Midsummer Night's Dream' by William Shakespeare (January 1997)
'Once Time' by Malcolm Hamilton (October 1996)
'An Baile's Strand' by W.B. Yeats (August 1996)

Recent Touring, Ireland
'A Midsummer Night's Dream' (1997, The Factory, Sligo; Black Box Theatre, Galway; The Granary, Cork; Garter Lane Theatre, Waterford; Samuel Beckett Centre, Dublin).

Recent Touring, Overseas
'A Midsummer Night's Dream' (1997, Riverside Studios, London)

Photo: Sandra O'Malley, John Carthy, Fiona McGeown, Ciaran McCauley, Liz Bracken and Kevin Collins in Blue Raincoat's production of 'Still Life'. ©James Connolly.

Calypso aims to push the boundaries of theatrical creativity by commissioning and producing high-profile, creative, innovative and new work that is relevant to the complex world it explores.

Recent Productions:
'Farawayan' (1998, The Olympic Ballroom, Dublin).
'Féile Fáilte' (1997, a theatrical parade from Temple Bar to the Civic Offices, Dublin).
'Rosie and Starwars' (1997, the Marquee at Meeting House Square, Temple Bar, Dublin).
'The Business of Blood' (1995, Project Arts Centre, Dublin).
'Trickledown Town' (1994, City Arts Centre).
'Hughie On The Wires' (1993, City Arts Centre, Dublin).

Recent Touring, Ireland:
'Farawayan' (Belfast, Cavan and Galway)
'Rosie and Starwars' (Ennis, Cork, Tuam, Ballybofey, Derry and Monaghan).
'Business Of Blood' (Waterford, Cork, Limerick, Derry and Galway).

Recent Touring, Overseas:
'Business Of Blood' (1995, London).
'Trickledown Town' (1994, Edinburgh and Glasgow).

Photo: Séamus Purcell astride the Celtic Tiger in 'Féile Fáilte'.
© Ronnie Close.

Calypso Productions

7 South Great Georges Street
Dublin 2
Tel: 01 6704539 / 6792236
Fax: 01 6704275
E-mail: calypso@tinet.ie

Admin contact: Antoinette O'Loughlin.
Artistic contact: Donal O'Kelly

Calypso was formed in November 1993 to make a positive social and theatrical contribution by creatively tackling issues that affect our lives and the lives of people around the world.

Centre Stage

99 Fitzroy Avenue
Belfast BT7 1HU
Tel: 01232 249119
Fax: 01232 283749
E-mail: cstage@argonet.co.uk
Web:http: //www.argonet.co.uk/users/cstage/

Admin contact: Roma Tomelty
Artistic contact: Colin Carnegie

Centre Stage is a Belfast based company which has been presenting professional productions since 1985. The company works to commissions and tours continuously. Centre Stage also hold classes and is a major supplier of workshops for community relations in primary schools.

The company's artistic policy is to present one major production of a play by an Ulster writer, working before 1969, annually and to stage international work that would otherwise not be seen in Northern Ireland.

Recent Productions:
'Bell, Book and Candle' by John Van Druten (1998, Riverside Theatre, Belfast). 'Henry Joy McCracken' by Jack Loudan (Riverside Theatre, Belfast; Belfast Arts Theatre). 'The Last Of The Red Hot Lovers' by Neil Simon (Riverside Theatre, Belfast; Europa Hotel, Belfast). 'The Evangelist' by Sam Thompson (Belfast Arts Theatre).

Recent Touring, Ireland:
'Henry Joy McCracken' (Hawk's Well Theatre, Sligo; Balor; Newry; Donaghmore; Riverside Theatre, Belfast; Omagh). 'The Wind And The Sleeping Harp' (Kilkenny Castle and most major Northern venues. 'Mischief and Madness' (most major Northern venues).

Recent Touring, Overseas:
'A Sublime Discord' (1997,Demarco Foundation, Edinburgh Festival). 'Schooled To A Foreign Voice' (Demarco Foundation, Edinburgh Festival). 'Take The Rising Road' (1994, E.E.C. Brussels).

Photo: A scene from Henry Joy McCracken by Jack Loudan. © Justin Conkey.

CoisCéim Dance Theatre

7 South Great Georges Street
Dublin 2
Tel: 01 6704134
Fax: 01 6704076
E-mail: coisceim@iol.ie
Website: homepages.iol.ie/~coisceim

Admin contact: Bridget Webster,
Company Manager
Artistic contact: David Bolger,
Artistic Director

CoisCéim is a dynamic dance theatre company which takes its name from the Irish word for *footstep*. Formed in 1995, CoisCéim has performed throughout Ireland, Scotland, London and in Marseilles. CoisCéim's mission is to produce high quality, accessible dance theatre in order to promote the awareness of, and increase the audiences for, contemporary dance in Ireland and of Irish contemporary dance overseas.

Recent Productions:
'Toupees and Snare Drums'.
'Ballads'.
'Back in Town'.
'Dragons and Tonics'.

Recent Touring, Ireland:
'Ballads'.
'Back in Town'.
'Dragons and Tonics'.

Recent Touring, Overseas:
'Back in Town'.
'Dragons and Tonics'.
'Straight with Curves'.

Photo: Muirne Bloomer, Aideen Gohery, Cindy Cummings and James Hosty in 'Toupees and Snare Drums'. © Kip Carroll

subsidised

Corcadorca Theatre Company Ltd

11 - 12 Marlboro Street, Cork.
Tel: 021 278326/087 2796058
Fax: 021 278326

Admin contact: Stephen Boyd,
General Manager
Artistic contact: Enda Walsh and
Pat Kiernan, Artistic Directors

Corcadorca has produced nineteen plays since it was founded in 1991. In Spring 1999 the company will stage the World Premiere of Enda Walsh's new play 'Misterman' in Cork before embarking on a tour. In Autumn 1999 Corcadorca will also stage a site specific production of 'The Merchant of Venice'.

Corcadorca sees itself using the potential of live theatre to electrify its audience, to reflect the concerns and feelings of the society from which that audience is drawn and to contribute to the enrichment of Cork's cultural life through the production of new theatre in new settings.

Recent Productions:
'Phaedra's Love' by Sarah Kane (1998, Irish Premiere 'Attica', Cork).
'Disco Pigs' by Enda Walsh. (1996, World Premiere, Triskel Arts Centre, Cork; 1997, Cork Opera House; 1998, Triskel Arts Centre).
'Animal Farm' (1996, Everyman Palace Theatre, Cork).
'Clockwork Orange' (1995, Sir Henry's, Cork).

Recent Touring, Ireland:
'Disco Pigs' (1996, Dublin Fringe Festiavl; 1997, Galway Arts Festival, Belfast Arts Festival, project @ the mint; 1998, Sligo Arts Festival).
'Ginger Ale Boy' (1996, Project Arts Centre, Belltable Arts Centre, Limerick).

Recent Touring, Overseas:
'Disco Pigs' (1997, Traverse Theatre, Edinburgh Festival, Bush Theatre, London; 1998 du Maurier World Stage, Toronto, Budapest, Arts Theatre, West End London, Bonn, Assembly Rooms, Edinburgh Festival, West Yorkshire Playhouse, Copenhagen Festival, Berlin Theatre Festival, Melbourne Festival, Adelaide Festival, Brighton Festival, Warwick Festival, Bristol Old Vic; 1999, Manchester).

Photo: Alison Mullin as Phaedra and Myles Horgan as Hypolytus in 'Phaedra's Love' by Sarah Kane. © Martin Healy.

Cork City Ballet

56 Clevedon
Kilmoney
Carrigaline
Co Cork
Tel: 021 375155
Fax: 021 375155

Admin contact: Janet Dillon
Artistic contact: Alan Foley

Cork City Ballet exists to provide a platform for Irish professional ballet dancers to perform. The company endeavours to produce new work, whilst re-producing ballets from our heritage of Irish National Ballet's repertoire.

Recent Productions:
'Le Corsaire Suite / Diverts' (March 1993).
'Ballet Spectactular' (March 1994).
'Ballet Spectactular' (April 1998).

Recent Touring, Ireland:
'Ballet For All' (1995).
'Ballet Spectactulor '96' (1996).

Recent Touring, Overseas:
'Willing and Able' (July 1996, London).
'Nutcracker' (Dec 1997, Isle of Man).

Photo: A Scene from Swan Lake © Roland Paschoff

The Corn Exchange

Unit 7
43/44 Temple Bar
Dublin 2
Tel: 01 6796444
Fax: 01 6796284
E-mail: cornexchange@tinet.ie

Admin contact: Kerry West
Artistic contact: Annie Ryan

The Corn Exchange was formed in 1995 by Annie Ryan. Since then it has been continually producing plays and running workshops. In 1998 the company received funding from The Arts Council.

The Corn Exchange is an umbrella organisation designed to develop, foster and produce theatre, dance and performance with the purpose of enriching the theatre community and deepening the performance experience.

Recent Productions

'Baby Jane' (1998, project @ the mint, Dublin).
'Big Bad Woolf' (1997, Temple Bar Gallary, Dublin Fringe Festival).
'Play On Two Chairs' (1997, Andrews Lane Theatre, Dublin Fringe Festival).
'Streetcar' (1996, Temple Bar Gallery, Dublin Fringe Festival).
Workshops in Commedia dell 'Arte, Long Form Improvisation and story theatre.

Recent Touring, Ireland:
'Play On Two Chairs' (1998, Old Museum Arts Centre, Belfast; Belltable Arts Centre, Limerick; Half Moon Theatre, Cork).

Recent Touring, Overseas:
'Play On Two Chairs' (1998, Edinburgh Fringe Festival)
'Play On Two Chairs' (1997, New York Fringe Festival)

Photo: Annie Ryan as Martha in 'Big Bad Woolf'.
© Paul McCarthy

The artistic policy of Daghdha embodies a commitment to developing the expression and understanding of modern dance as a vital element of human communication. Daghdha's primary focus is the creation of original choreographic works which have a unique movement aesthetic and are visually and dramatically stimulating.

Daghdha Dance Company

University of Limerick
Limerick
Tel: 061 202804 / 202943
Fax: 061 331304/330316
E-mail: daghdha@ul.ie
Web: http://www.ul.ie/~ddc

Admin contact: Bridget Cleary
Artistic contact: Mary Nunan

Founded in 1988 by Mary Nunan, Daghdha Dance Company is a professional modern dance theatre company whose primary focus is the creation of original choreographic works which have a unique movement aesthetic, and are kinetically exciting and visually stimulating. Daghdha produces two dance programmes annually - a theatre programme and an education programme. The Company has toured extensively both nationally and internationally to much critical acclaim.

Recent Theatre Productions
'Chimera' (October 1998).
'Here Then - Elsewhere Now' (May 1997).
'Aerdha' (September 1996).
'On Earth As It Is In Heaven' (March 1996).

Recent Touring, Ireland:
'Chimera' (October 1998).
'3 Piece Suite', comprising 'Here Then - Elsewhere Now', 'Aerdha' and 'On Earth As It Is In Heaven' (June 1997).
'Here Then - Elsewhere Now' (May 1997, Great Irish Famine Event).
'New Twist' (for young audiences) (Dublin, Cork, Limerick and Northern Ireland).

Recent Touring, Overseas:
'Chimera' (October 1998, Festival International Cervantino, Mexico).
Video production of 'Territorial Claims' (December 1997, Dance on Camera Festival, New York; June 1998, Naples, Italy).
'Territorial Claims' and 'Fictional' (Galve, Sweeden; Pompidou Centre, Paris).
'New Twist' (Suffolk, England).

*Photo: Diane Bourgain in 'Here Then - Elsewhere Now',
Choreography: Mary Nunan. © Arthur Gough.*

Dance Theatre of Ireland

13 Clarinda Park North
Dun Laoghaire, Co Dublin
Tel: 01 2803455
Fax: 01 2803466
E-mail: danceire@iol.ie

Admin contact: Orla O'Doherty,
Administrator
Artistic contact: Robert Connor,
Loretta Yurick, Artistic Directors

Founded in 1989, Dance Theatre of Ireland performs the work of Robert Connor and Loretta Yurick as well as selected international and Irish choreographers. The Company tours internationally featuring collaborations with major Irish composers and designers.

The company's artistic policy is to create, perform and tour dance works which are human in content, original in form and strong in theatrical and emotional impact. Through Dancepop the company also runs an innovative and popular educational outreach programme of workshops accompanying all performances - over 21,900 participants to date.

Recent Productions
'Tombs' (1997/98).
'Jours Etranges / Like Water Flowing East' (1997).
'Body Travels Time / Deseo' (1996).
'Bonefire and Deserts D'Amour' (1995).

Recent Touring, Ireland
1998 - Town Hall Theatre, Galway; Hawk's Well Theatre, Sligo; Belltable Arts Centre, Limerick; Watergate Theatre, Kilkenny; Firkin Crane Arts Centre, Cork; Tivoli Theatre, Dublin; Bru Na Boinne Visitor Centre, Dun Laoghaire County Hall, Jobstown Community Centre, NUI Maynooth Hall, Kildare; Waterfront Theatre, Belfast; Ardhowen Theatre, Enniskillen; Riverside Theatre, Coleraine).
1997 - Backstage Theatre, Longford; Rialto Theatre, Derry; Tivoli Theatre, Dublin; Galway and Limerick).
1996 - Opera House, Cork; Longford, Kilkenny, and Limerick).

Recent Touring, Overseas:
1998 - Lak Theatre, Leiden & Bellevue Theatre, Amsterdam, The Netherlands.
1996 - Montpellier International Danse Festival; The Place Theatre, London.
1995 - Kristineham Festival, Sweden.

Photo: Inge Buyls and JJ Formento in 'Tombs'.
© Tony Higgins.

Recent Productions:
'The Lonesome West' by Martin McDonagh (July 1998).
'Philadelphia, Here I Come!' by Brian Friel (March 1998).
'The Leenane Trilogy' by Martin McDonagh (June 1997).
'Shoot The Crow' by Owen McCafferty (February 1997).

Druid Theatre Company

Druid Lane
Galway
Tel: 091 568660 / 568617
Fax: 091 563109

Admin contact:
Louise Donlon/Maria Fleming
Artistic contact: Garry Hynes

Druid is a professional theatre company, based in Galway city, which was founded in 1975. Based at its own venue in Galway, Druid Lane, the company also tours extensively in Ireland and abroad.

The company has in recent years focused mainly on new Irish writing, bringing the works of Tom Murphy, Frank McGuinness, Vincent Woods and Martin McDonagh to the stage. Druid has also embarked on a series of large-scale projects, including 'The Leenane Trilogy' in June 1997 and the forthcoming Synge Festival.

Recent Touring, Ireland:
'Philadelphia, Here I Come!' (Limerick and Longford).
'A Skull in Connemara' by Martin McDonagh (Tralee, Skibbereen, Sligo, Belfast, Armagh, Longford, Wexford, Cork and Limerick).
'The Leenane Trilogy' (transferred to London's Royal Court Theatre before an Irish tour of Cork, Galway and Dublin).

Recent Touring, Overseas:
'The Beauty Queen of Leenane' (currently running at the Walter Kerr Theatre, on Broadway, having transferred from the Atlantic Theatre Company off-Broadway in April 1998, where it had been playing since February 1998).
'The Leenane Trilogy' (January 1998, Sydney Festival; July/August 1997, The Royal Court Theatre, Downstairs, London).

Photo: Dawn Bradfield and Andrew Scott in 'The Lonesome West' play 3 of 'The Leenane Trilogy' by Martin McDonagh. © Amelia Stein.

Dubbeljoint Productions

245 Lisburn Road
Belfast BT9 7EN
Tel: 01232 202222
Fax: 01232 202223
E-mail: vinmccann@yahoo.com

Admin contact: Vincent McCann
Artistic contact: Pam Brighton

Dubbeljoint was established in 1991 by Pam Brighton, Marie Jones and Mark Lambert. Since its inception the company has premiered at least one new play per year.

The Company's artistic policy is to create and perform plays which will be enjoyed by and which will be attractive to as many people as possible throughout Northern Ireland and further afield.

Recent Productions:
'The Mother Of All The Behans' by Peter Sheridan.
'A Moon For The Misbegotten' by Eugene O'Neill.
'Binlids' by Justus Community Theatre.
'Stones In His Pockets' by Marie Jones.

Recent Touring, Ireland:
'The Mother Of All The Behans' by Peter Sheridan.
'A Moon For The Misbegotten' by Eugene O'Neill.
'Stones In His Pockets' by Marie Jones.

Recent Touring, Overseas:
'A Night In November'.

Photo: John Hewitt as Phil Hogan and Sean Campion as Jim Tyrone in 'A Moon for the Misbegotten'. © Christopher Hill Photographic.

Fabulous Beast Dance Theatre was conceived in February 1997, by Michael Keegan Dolan, choreographer; Mick Dolan, dancer and Jenny Roche, dancer. All three are Irish and met while studying together at The Central School of Ballet, London, from 1988 - 1991.

The company's artistic policy is to reinvent dance theatre by creating highly theatrical, beautifully crafted work using themes which lend themselves to this magical and highly physical medium. Audience needs are the company's priority.

Fabulous Beast Dance Theatre

19 Kincora Grove
Clontarf
Dublin 3
Tel: 01 8336682/ 0171 2881296 (London)
Fax: 0171 2881296 (London only)

Contact: Michael Keegan Dolan

Recent Productions:
'The Good People' (1998, commissioned by Firkin Crane's New Works Series).
'Sunday Lunch' (1997, commissioned by Firkin Crane's New Works Series).

Recent Touring, Ireland:
The Firkin Crane, Cork (1997/98).
Samuel Beckett Centre, Dublin (1998).

Photo: Jenny Roche and Mike Dolan in 'The Good People' co-production with Firkin Crane. © Derek Speirs / Report.

Through its New Works Series commissions Firkin Crane presents the best of contemporary Irish and International dance companies between the months of September and June annually.

Firkin Crane

Shandon
Co Cork
Tel: 021 507487
Fax: 021 501124

Admin contact: Ger O'Riordan
Artistic contact: Mary Brady

Firkin Crane presents its New Work Series by invitation, showcasing works by prominent Irish or Irish based independent choreographers. Solo Independents show cases female dance artists in celebration of International Womens Day.

Recent Productions

'Sunday Lunch' - (1997, with Fabulous Beast, commissioned by Firkin Crane's New Works Series)
'Good People' - (1997, with Fabulous Beast, commissioned by Firkin Crane's New Works Series)
Solo Independents (1997)
Solo Independents (1998)

Recent Touring, Ireland

'Good People' and 'Sunday Lunch' - (1998, Dublin Fringe Festival).

Photo: Adriene Brown, Judith Sibley and Fergus O'Conchuir in 'Time Out Project'. © F22 Photography.

Fishamble Theatre Company Ltd

Shamrock Chambers
1-2 Eustace Street
Dublin 2
Tel: 01 6704018
Fax: 01 6704019
E-Mail: fishamble@isite.ie
Admin contact: Maureen Kennelly
Artistic contact: Jim Culleton

Fishamble (formerly Pigsback) has produced many award-winning plays by emerging and established playwrights. Plans include new plays by Joe O'Connor and Gavin Kostick, as well as a festival of short plays to celebrate the new millennium.

Fishamble is committed to developing innovative new Irish writing for the theatre, and to presenting this original work in exciting, dynamic productions to audiences in Ireland and overseas.

Recent Productions:
'The Nun's Wood' by Pat Kinevane (1998, project @ the mint, Dublin).
'From Both Hips' by Mark O'Rowe (1997, project @ the mint, Dublin).
'The Flesh Addict' by Gavin Kostick (1996, Temple Bar Music Centre, Dublin Theatre Festival).
'Sardines' by Michael West (1995, Samuel Beckett Centre, Dublin Theatre Festival)

Recent Touring, Ireland:
'The Nun's Wood' (1998 Backstage Theatre, Longford; Watergate Theatre, Kilkenny; Belltable Arts Centre, Limerick; Opera House, Cork).
'The Flesh Addict' (1996, Galway Arts Centre, Galway; Garage Theatre, Monaghan; Belltable Arts Centre, Limerick; Backstage Theatre, Longford; Watergate Theatre, Kilkenny).
'Red Roses and Petrol' by Joe O'Connor (1995, Hawk's Well Theatre, Sligo; Belltable Arts Centre, Limerick; Galway Arts Centre, Galway; Garter Lane Arts Centre, Waterford).

Recent Touring, Overseas:
'From Both Hips' (1997, Tron Theatre, Glasgow).
'Red Roses and Petrol' (1995, Tricycle Theatre, London).
'The Ash Fire' (1993, Traverse Theatre, Edinburgh; Tricycle Theatre, London; Mayfest, Glasgow)

Photo: Emily Nagle and Fiona Condon in 'The Nun's Wood' by Pat Kinevane. © Colm Henry.

Focus Theatre Company

6 Pembroke Place
off Upper Pembroke Street
Dublin 2
Tel: 01 6763071 / 6607109
Fax: 01 6607109

Admin contact: Mary Jude Ryan,
Administrator
Artistic contact: Deirdre O'Connell,
Artistic Director

Focus opened in 1967 under the direction of Deirdre O'Connell. It seats 60 people and is also the home of the famous Stanislavski Studio where Deirdre O'Connell teaches 'the method'. There is a small theatre board who takes a vital advisory role.

The company's artistic policy is to present plays of merit not commonly known in Ireland and to provide for the stimulation and assistance of dramatic writing and to provide comprehensive theatrical training.

Recent Productions:
'The Watchman' by Seán Lawlor.
'Anna Christie' by Eugene O'Neill.
'Jordan' by Anna Reynolds and Moira Buffini.
'Playing Sinatra' by Bernard Kops.

Photo: Stephanie Dunne, Robert McDowell and Michelle Costello in 'Healing the Dead' by Johnny Hanrahan. © Tommy Clancy.

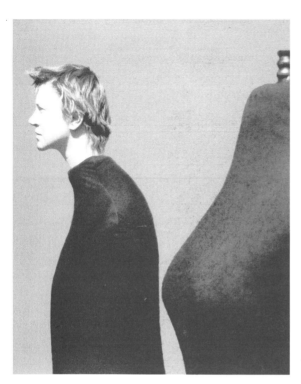

Galloglass was founded in 1990 with a view to producing high quality modern theatre for touring from a permanent base in Clonmel, Co. Tipperary. Since its establishment, Galloglass has pursued an non-naturalistic aesthetic and dedicated itself to touring. Tours average 10 weeks; regular touring circuit includes regional towns and cities in Southern and Northern Ireland, Dublin, Belfast and several towns in Wales.

Recent Productions:
'The Crack and the Whip' by Colin Teevan (Autumn 1997).
'Stir It Up' by Madeline Dewhurst (Spring 1997 & 1998).
'Broken Ground' a devised play scripted by Sylvia Cullen (Winter 1997).
'An Ideal Husband' by Oscar Wilde (Summer 1996).

Recent Touring, Ireland:
'Breathing Space' a devised play scripted by Ken Bourke, co-produced with Welsh Company Theatre West Glamorgan. This show is playing a limited number of performances in Ireland and Wales in Autumn 1998. It is scheduled to do an extensive tour in the Summer / Autumn 1999.

Photo: Gabriel Reidy in 'Breathing Space' scripted by Ken Bourke. © Ioan Hesin.

Galloglass Theatre Company

30 Parnell Street
Clonmel
Co Tipperary
Tel: 052 26797
Fax: 052 27270
E-mail: gallo@iol.ie

Admin contact: David Teevan, Company Manager; Corina Morrisey, Administrator
Artistic contact: Theresia Guschlbauer

The Gate maintains a high profile overseas while pursuing a standard of excellence in producing new Irish plays and Irish and European classics at home.

Recent Productions:
Anton Chekhov's 'Uncle Vanya' a new version by Brian Friel.
'The Weir' by Conor McPherson.
'A Streetcar Named Desire' by Tennessee Williams.
'Long Day's Journey Into Night' by Eugene O'Neill.

Recent Touring, Ireland:
'Catalpa' by Donal O'Kelly - Limerick and Kilkenny.
'Great Expectations' - Belfast Opera House.
'Waiting For Godot' by Samuel Beckett - Kilkenny.

Recent Touring, Overseas:
'Lady Windermere's Fan' (May / June 1998, Spoleto Festival, Charleston, South Carolina).
Four Beckett plays and 'Catalpa' (Oct 1997 Melbourne International Festival for the Arts).
Beckett Festival (1996, all 19 of Beckett's plays - The Lincoln Centre Festival, New York).

The Gate Theatre

Cavendish Row, Dublin 1
Tel: 01 8744368 / 8744085
Fax: 01 8745373

Contact: Michael Colgan, Director

The Gate Theatre was founded in 1928 and became internationally renowned as one of the most adventurous and far-sighted play houses in Europe.

In December 1983, Michael Colgan became Director of the Gate and highlights of the Gate's programme since then include 'I'll Go On', 'Juno and the Paycock', 'Three Sisters', The Beckett Festival and The Pinter Festival, together with new plays by leading contemporary playwrights.

Photo: Barry McGovern as 'Vladimir' in 'Waiting for Godot' by Samuel Beckett. © Tom Lawlor.

Graffiti Theatre Company

The Weighmaster's House
2 Church Street
Shandon
Cork
Tel: 021 397111
Fax: 021 397110
E-mail: graffiti@tinet.ie

Admin contact: Jennifer O'Donnell
Artistic contact: Emelie Fitzgibbon

Graffiti Theatre Company has been providing top quality theatre for young audiences for over fourteen years. In that time the company's Theatre In Education productions have been seen by over 400,000 young people in every part of Ireland. Graffiti's productions have been praised both at home and abroad for their high standards, originality and excellence as they seek to achieve the ideal balance between entertainment and education.

The company's artistic policy is to provide a permanent, professional, educational theatre company to the Munster and South Leinster area. To provide a service, to the youth of the company's community by extending the range and availability of children's and young people's theatre and workshops.

Recent Productions:
'Forget Me Not' by Graffiti Theatre Company.
'The Maze of Power' by Soren Skjold.
'The Changeling' by Graffiti Theatre Company.
'Jackie's Day' by Sarah FitzGibbon.

Recent Touring, Ireland:
All the company's productions tour schools in Munster and South Leinster.

Recent Touring, Overseas:
'The Riddle Keeper' by Laurie Brooks Gollobin (1996, Wales and Scotland).
'Forget Me Not' (1997, France and Coventry).
'The Maze of Power' (November 1997,Sweden).

Photo: Evanna O'Meara and Diane O'Keefe in 'The Changeling'. © Derek Speirs.

Island Theatre Company

Church Street
King's Island
Limerick
Tel: 061 410433
Fax: 061 400997
E-mail: islandtc@indigo.ie

Admin contact: Conor Nolan
Artistic contact: Terry Devlin

Island Theatre Company's general policy is to explore the tensions of being Irish today through the medium of performance. The company's approach involves an aggressive interaction with the text to create a stimulating and entertaining production.

The company hopes to tour to Britain in 1999.

Recent Productions:
'Borrowed Robes' by John Barrett (July/August 1998, Belltable Arts Centre, Limerick)
'A Midsummer Night's Dream' by William Shakespeare (June/July 1997, St. Mary's Cathedral, Limerick).
'The Ante Room' adapted by Kevin O'Conner (July/August 1996, Belltable Arts Centre, Limerick).
'The Coleen Bawn' by Dion Boucicault (July/August 1995, Belltable Arts Centre, Limerick)

Recent Touring, Ireland:
'Borrowed Robes' by John Barrett (1998, regional tour).
'Bouncers' by John Goodbar (1996, regional tour).

Recent Touring, Overseas
Hope to tour to Britain in 1999.

Photo: John Anthony Murphy as Fr. Keane in 'Borrowed Robes'. © Arthur Gough.

Founded in 1991, John Scott's Irish Modern Dance Theatre has created 16 original works. The company has toured to over 30 venues throughout Ireland and performed internationally in France and Sweden.

The company's artistic policy is to promote the creation of new works by living choreographers both Irish and international to develop and enlighten the audience for modern dance in Ireland and abroad through extensive touring and workshops.

John Scott's Irish Modern Dance Theatre

37 North Great Georges Street
Dublin 1
Tel: 01 8749616
Fax: 01 8787784
E-mail: imdt@iol.ie
Website: http://www.adnet.ie/imdt

Admin contact: Marina Rafter
Artistic contact: John Scott

Recent Productions:
'Real Pearls' (1998).
'Nous - The Loss Of The Winds' (1997).
'Just bodies' (1997).
'You Must Tell The Bees' (1996).

Recent Touring, Ireland:
'Real Pearls' (1998).
'Just Bodies' (1997).
'You Must Tell The Bees' (1996).

Recent Touring, Overseas:
'Real Pearls' (1998, Sweden).
'Just Bodies' (1998, Paris; 1997, Sweden).
'Nous - The Loss Of The Winds' (1998, Paris).

Photo: Justine Doswell, Lucy Dundon, Johnathan Mitchell & Daryn Crosbie. © Chris Nash.

Kabosh's artistic policy is to produce work inspired by the screen, crafted for the stage. Igniting imagination, Stimulating new ideas and innovation, Exciting audiences through new presentation and Educating those through access to live theatre (I.S.E.E.).

Recent Productions:
'Northern Exposures' (August 1998).
'Hansel and Grettel' (December 1997).
'Rumpelstilskin' (November - December 1997).
'Misery' (October - November 1997).
Belfast City Arts Award Nominee 1998.

Recent Touring, Ireland:
'Mojo Mickybo' by Owen McCafferty (1998, all Ireland tour).
'Misery' (1997, all Ireland tour).
'Torch Song Trilogy' (1996, all Ireland tour)
'Freefalling' by Owen McCafferty (1996).

Recent Touring, Overseas:
'Talking Heads' by Alan Bennett (1995, Spanish Tour)
'Freefalling' by Owen McCafferty (1996, Edinburgh Fringe Festival). Winner Little Devil Award Best Play

Photo: Anne Bird as Annie Wilks and Richard Croxford as Paul Sheldon in 'Misery' by Simon Moore. © Derry Journal 1997.

Kabosh Productions Ltd.

Old Museum Arts Centre
7 College Square North
Belfast BT1 6AR
Tel: 01232 243343
Fax: 01232 243343

Admin contact: Tania Carlisle, Administrator
Artistic contact: Karl Wallace, Artistic Director

Loose Canon Theatre Company

43 Morehampton Road
Donnybrook
Dublin 4
Tel: 01 6606012
Fax: 01 6606012
E-mail: loosecan@indigo.ie
Admin contact: Willie White
Artistic contact: Jason Byrne

Founded in 1996. Working with classical texts, Loose Canon aims to pursue an ascetic style of presentation which places its emphasis on performance.

Future plans include 'The White Devil' at project @ the mint, Dublin in January 1999.

Recent Productions:
'Coriolanus' by William Shakespeare (March 1998, project @ the mint, Dublin).
'The Spanish Tragedy' by Thomas Kyd (Sept. 1997, project @ the mint, Dublin).
'The Duchess of Malfi' by John Webster (June 1997, Crypt Arts Centre, Dublin Castle).
'Measure for Measure' by William Shakespeare (Oct 1996, City Arts Centre, Dublin).

Photo: (Left to Right) Conan Sweeny, Robert Shaw, Mark D'Aughton, Jonathan Byrne and Paschal Friel in 'Coriolanus' by William Shakespeare. © Amelia Stein.

subsidised

Lyric Theatre Belfast

55 Ridgeway Street
Belfast BT9 5FB
Tel: 01232 669660
Fax: 01232 381395
E-mail: rgaston@lyrictheatre.co.uk
Website: http://www.lyrictheatre.co.uk

Admin contact: Patricia McBride
Artistic contact: David Grant

The Lyric Players was founded in 1951 by Mary O'Malley. The Lyric Theatre opened in 1968 and is Northern Ireland's only full time repertory theatre, with former Lyric actor Liam Neeson as patron.

The Lyric has a particular commitment to the classics, work by Irish writers, the commissioning and presentation of new plays, and co-productions with local theatre companies.

Recent Productions
'Little Shop Of Horrors' (July 1998).
'Translations' (April 1998).
'Tearing The Loom' (March 1998).
'Miss Julie' (February 1998).

Recent Touring, Ireland:
'Translations' (May 1998, Armagh, Downpatrick, Derry and Coleraine).
'Jane Eyre' (May 1997, Derry and Enniskillen).
'Pygmalion' (March 1997, throughout the North of Ireland and Galway).

Recent Touring, Overseas:
'Philadelphia, Here I Come!' (1996, U.S.A. tour).
'Ghosts' (1990, Oslo, Norway tour).

Photo: Lyric Theatre, Belfast. © Chris Hill Photographic.

The Machine

Hilltown
Dunboyne
Co. Meath
Tel: 01 8255395
Fax: 01 8255395
E-mail: scottart@tinet.ie
Website: http://homepage.tinet.ie/~sfa

Admin contact: Avril Ryan
Artistic contact: Michael Scott

1998 marks fourteen years in operation for The Machine. In the last two years the company has produced 'The Yellow Man', 'The Cuchulain Cycle' on three separate occasions, 'Dracula' and 'Something About Us'. Later this year The Machine will produce 'Purgatory', a new opera by Michael Scott from the play by W.B. Yeats.

The driving force behind The Machine work is the integration of European theatre methods into the fabric of Irish Theatre making. To this end the company has worked not only in major theatres but within close knit communities both in Dublin and throughout the country, on both sides of the border. The company works not only in the area of theatre but also in film, music, dance and providing arts related administrative services. The company is also in the process of developing its own theatre website 'The Irish Theatre Resource' which provides listing and information links on Irish and international theatre.

Recent Productions:
'The Cuchulain Cycle' by W.B. Yeats (RHA Downstairs, Dublin and Riverside Studios, London).
'Dracula' by Bram Stoker adapted by Michael Scott (RHA Downstairs, Dublin).
'The Rocky Horror Show' co-produced with MCD (Olympia Theatre, Dublin).
'Something About Us' by Andrew Alty (RHA Downstairs, Dublin).

Recent Touring, Overseas
'The Cuchulain Cycle' by W.B. Yeats / Music by Michael Scott / additional music Avril Ryan (1998, Riverside Studios in Hammersmith, London).

Photo: Aidan Condron (Michael) & Alan Devine (Peter) in
'Something About Us' by Andrew Alty. © Amelia Stein.

Macnas' artistic policy is to have fun on a grand scale and to create a climate for participation in the arts.

Recent Productions:
'Diamonds In The Soil' (1998, Dublin Theatre Festival).
'The Dead School' by Patrick McCabe (July 1998, co-production with Galway Arts Festival).
'Balor'.
'Rhymes From The Ancient Mariner'.

Recent Touring, Ireland:
'Diamonds In The Soil' (Autumn 1998).
'Balor' (Autumn 1996).
'Sweeny' (1994).

Recent Touring, Overseas:
'Balor' (U.S.A., Columbia, Scotland).
'Sweeny' (U.S.A., France).
'Tain' (Spain and the U.K.).

Macnas

Fisheries Field
Salmon Weir Bridge
Galway
Tel: 091 561462
Fax: 091 563905
E-mail: macnas@iol.ie
Website: http://www.failte.com/macnas

Admin contact: Declan Gibbons, General Manager

Macnas is a community arts and theatre company. Based in Galway but travelling widely, Macnas creates theatre indoors and on the streets and works in schools and in local communities.

Photo: 'Diamonds in the Soil'.

Based in Cork, Meridian has been mounting shows since 1989, many of them incorporating various musical idioms. The artistic partnership of playwright Johnny Hanrahan and composer John Browne is at the heart of the company's work. This has resulted in a series of productions in which live music, ensemble playing and experimental use of technology have marked out a particular Meridian style.

The company's artistic policy is essentially concerned with the presentation of challenging content in accessible theatrical forms.

Recent Productions:
'Craving' (Everyman Palace Theatre, Cork).
'Reading Turgenev' (Everyman Palace Theatre, Cork).
'The Cavalcaders' (Everyman Palace Theatre, Cork).
'Trios' (Granary Theatre, Cork).

Meridian Theatre Company

11/12 Marlboro Street
Cork
Tel: 021 276837
Fax: 021 279134
E-mail: meridtc@iol.ie

Admin contact: Deirdre McCarthy
Artistic contact: Johnny Hanrahan

Recent Touring, Ireland:
'Craving' (1998).
'Reading Turgenev' (1997).
'The Cavalcaders' (1996).

Photo: Franke Bourke as John Paul and Elizabeth Moynihan as Aisling in 'Craving' by Johnny Hanrahan and John Browne. © Tom Lawlor.

The National Theatre Society Limited

comprising of both The Abbey and Peacock Theatres.

The Abbey and Peacock Theatres
26 Lower Abbey Street, Dublin 1
Tel: 01 8748741
Fax: 01 8729177
Artistic contact: Patrick Mason
Admin contact: Martin Fahy

The Abbey Theatre opened in 1904, merging the literary talents of WB Yeats, Lady Augusta Gregory and Edward Martyn with the acting experience of the Fay brothers, to form the Irish National Theatre Society. The society comprises of two theatres, The Abbey and Peacock, and features the work of playwrights such as Brian Friel, Tom Murphy, Frank McGuinness, O'Casey, Behan, Yeats, Synge and Shaw, as well as fostering new writing by Sebastian Barry, Dermot Bolger and Marina Carr.

The National Theatre Society's artistic policy is to develop and promote Irish theatre artists, to keep alive the repertoire of Irish classic plays, to encourage and foster new Irish writing talent, and to present high quality productions of International and European classics.

Recent Productions: *Abbey Theatre:*
'The Colleen Bawn' by Dion Boucicault.
'Saint Joan' by Bernard Shaw.
'Kevin's Bed' by Bernard Farrell.
'Juno and the Paycock' by Sean O'Casey.
Peacock Theatre:
'At Swin-Two-Birds' by Flann O'Brien. New adaptation by Alex Johnston.
'As The Beast Sleeps' by Gary Mitchell.
'Caoineadh Airt Uí Laoghaire' by Tom Mac Intyre.
'The Electrocution of Children' by Chris Lee.

Recent Touring, Ireland:
'Caoineadh Airt Uí Laoghaire' by Tom Mac Intyre (1998, Gaeltacht Tour).
'In A Little World Of Our Own' by Gary Mitchell (1997, National Tour).
'Sour Grapes' by Michael Harding (1997, National Tour).

Recent Touring, Overseas:
'The Secret Fall of Constance Wilde' by Thomas Kilroy (Melbourne Festival, Australia).
'Tarry Flynn' by Patrick Kavanagh new adaptation by Conall Morrison (The Lyttleton, National Theatre of Great Britain).
'Observe The Sons Of Ulster Marching Towards The Somme' by Frank McGuinness (The Barbican, London, Blackpool, Liverpool, Plymouth, Belfast, Paris, Brussels and Bonn).

Photo: James Kennedy and Pauline Flannagan in 'Tarry Flynn'.
© Amelia Stein.

Excellence and accessibility are the company's main artistic aims, with an innovative approach to traditional repertoire and a serious commitment to modern work and new Irish commissions.

Recent Productions:
'Cinderella' by Peter Maxwell Davies (September / October 1998).
'The Lighthouse' by Peter Maxwell Davies (July / August 1998).
'Così fan tutte' by W.A. Mozart (February 1998).
'The Magic Flute' by W.A. Mozart (November / December 1997).

Opera Theatre Company

Temple Bar Music Centre
Curved Street
Temple Bar
Dublin 2
Tel: 01 6794962
Fax: 01 6794963
E-mail: otc@imn.ie
Website: http://www.imn.ie/otc

Admin contact: James Conway
Artistic contact: James Conway

Opera Theatre Company was established in 1986 with the remit of touring quality opera nationwide. Since then it has toured an average three productions per year of traditional and modern repertoire.

Recent Touring, Ireland:
'Cinderella' (1998, Dublin, Gorey, Kilkenny, New Ross, Longford, Cavan, Westport, Drogheda, Ballinteer, Ballyshannon, Enniskillen and Limerick).
'The Lighthouse' (1998, Longford, Ennis, Galway, Dublin, Sligo, Boyle, Belfast, New Ross and Kerry).
'Così fan tutte' (Galway, Sligo, Derry, Dundalk, Dublin, Athlone, Limerick, Tralee and Cork).

Recent Touring, Overseas:
'Katya Kabonova' by Janacek (March 1998, Expo '98 - 100 days festival).
'Tamerlano' by Handel (February 1998, Expo '98 - 100 days festival).
'My Love, My Umbrella' by Conway / O'Connell (6 - Tage Opera Fest, Dusseldorf).

Photo: (Left to Right) Sam McElroy, John Milne and Eugene Gurity in 'The Lighthouse'. © Vincent Sneyd.

Operating Theatre

c/o Shamrock Chambers
1/2 Eustace Street
Dublin 2
Tel: 01 6704018
Fax: 01 6704019

Admin contact: Maureen Kennelly
Artistic contact: Roger Doyle /
Olwen Fouere

Operating Theatre was initiated by Roger Doyle and Olwen Fouere in 1981 as a music and theatre company with the aim of producing innovative forms of theatre in which music is a core element. The company will present 'Angel / Babel' at project @ the mint in Dublin in March 1999 and is keen to tour this production.

Recent Productions:
'The Diamond Body' (1988).
'The Pentagonal Dream' (1986).

Recent Touring, Overseas:
'The Diamond Body' (London, Glasgow, Avignon and Caracas).

Photo: Olwen Fouere in 'Pentagonal Dream'. © Amelia Stein.

Pan Pan Theatre Company

The Old School House, Eblana Avenue
Dun Laoghaire, Co Dublin
Tel: 01 2800544
Fax: 01 2300918
E-mail: panpan@iol.ie
Website: http://www.iol.ie/~panpan
Admin contact: Mary O'Donovan
Artistic contact: Gavin Quinn

Pan Pan Theatre Company was set up in 1993 by Aedin Cosgrove and Gavin Quinn. It has produced eight original productions which have been toured widely both in Ireland (north and south) and in Europe.

Pan Pan Theatre aims for innovation as well as developing what is best in our theatrical tradition. Pan Pan also aims to tour work nationally and internationally, developing links with the audiences they are performing for. Pan Pan Theatre will produce the 3rd Dublin International Theatre Symposium between 11th - 16th January 1999 at the Samuel Beckett Centre, Trinity College, Dublin.

Recent Productions:
'Cartoon' (October 1998, project @ the mint, Dublin). 'Peepshow' (1997, Samuel Beckett Centre as part of the 2nd Dublin International Theatre Symposium; June 1998, Samuel Beckett Centre) 'Tailors Requiem' (1996, project @ the mint as part of the Dublin Theatre Festival) 'A Bronze Twist Of Your Serpent Muscles' (1995, Winner of Best Overall Production Dublin Fringe Festival 1995)

Recent Touring, Ireland
'A Bronze Twist Of Your Serpent Muscles' (Eight venues in Ireland and Northern Ireland). 'Tailors Requiem' (Limerick, Drogheda, Sligo Arts Festival, Omagh, Dun Laoighaire-Rathdown, Derry, Belfast, Monaghan and Listowel).

Recent Touring, Overseas:
1998 - Invisible Cities Festival in Stockholm, Brouhaha International Festival in Liverpool. 'Cartoon' (International Theatre Festival in Lublin, Poland). 'Peepshow' (1997, Millennium Festival in Gdansk; Olstzyn, Poland; Waggonhall in Marburg, Germany; The International Cultural Centre in Ultrecht, The Netherlands.) 'Tailors Requiem' (1996, Brest as part of L'Imaginaire Irlandais; Edinburgh Fringe Festival; Theatre Days Festival, Riksteatern, Stockholm, Sweden; The Spectrum Festival in Villach, Austria). 'A Bronze Twist Of Your Serpent Muscles' (1996, La Friche la Belle de Mai, Marseilles as part of the L'Imaginaire Irlandais Festival).

Recent Productions:
'Native City' (1998, Tivoli Theatre).
'Fully Recovered' (1998, project @ the mint, Dublin).
'Massive Damages' (1997, Tivoli Theatre, Dublin).
'Kitchensink' (1996/97, Andrews Lane Theatre, Dublin and Tivoli Theatre, Dublin).

Recent Touring, Ireland:
'Massive Damages' (1997, Limerick, Cork, Kilkenny, Sligo & Galway).
'Kitchensink' (1996/97, Cork, Galway, Sligo, Kilkenny, Tralee, Carrigallen, Limerick).
'Too Much Too Young' (1995, Cork).

Touring Overseas:
'Kitchensink' (1997, Tricycle Theatre, London; Thessaloniki, Greece).
'Buddleia' (1996, Donmar Warehouse, London; Kontakt Festival, Poland).
'Studs' (1992/93 Edinburgh, Liverpool, London).

Photo: 'Kitchensink', © Derek Speirs.

The Passion Machine

30 Gardiner Place
Dublin 1
Tel: 01 8788857
Fax: 01 8788845

Admin contact: Anne Gately
Artistic contact: Paul Mercier

Founded in 1984, The Passion Machine produces only original work and has, to date, produced 27 new Irish plays. The company is funded by the Arts Council of Ireland and is sponsored by Yamanouchi (Ire).

Prime Cut's artistic policy is to produce and promote contemporary international drama and to actively encourage and create partnerships and exchanges with fellow international practitioners.

Recent Productions:
'Brilliant Traces' by Cindy Lou Johnson.
'Stone & Ashes' by Daniel Danis.
'Simpatico' by Sam Sheperd.
'Who Shall Be Happy...?' by Trevor Griffiths.

Recent Touring, Ireland:
Three of the above productions have toured to Belfast and Dublin, 'Simpatico' also toured extensively throughout Ireland. 'Brilliant Traces' will be revived in January 1999 for a three month tour of Ireland, including the Lyric Theatre, Belfast and the project @ the mint, Dublin.

Recent Touring, Overseas
'Who Shall Be Happy...?' toured internationally, performing as part of the Irish Arts Festival of Aarhus in Denmark, at the West Yorkshire Playhouse, Leeds and a month's residency at the Bush Theatre, London. Currently involved with Tinderbox in co-ordinating a cultural exchange between playwrights from Quebec and Ireland which will involve a Festival of new work being presented in both Montreal and Belfast.

Photo: Lalor Roddy and Michelle Fairleigh in 'Death and the Maiden'. © Jill Jennings.

Prime Cut Productions

404 McAvoy House
17a Ormeau Avenue
Belfast BT2 8HD
Tel: 01232 313156
Fax: 01232 313156
E-mail: primecut.cbn@artservicesireland.com
Website: www.artservicesireland.com/cbn

Admin contact: Sean Kelly
Artistic contact: Jackie Doyle

Prime Cut produce 2 to 3 full scale productions a year (at least one of which is a touring show). The company is also involved in co-producing and international exchange schemes.

Project exists in order to encourage and foster emerging and established artists to create new and innovative work in a contemporary context.

Recent Productions:
'A Border Worrier' by John Byrne (1997, project @ the mint, Dublin).
'The Gay Detective' by Gerard Stembridge (1996, Project Arts Centre).
'Come Good Rain' by George Seremba (1996, Project Arts Centre).
'Sapa' with CRISUS (USA) (1996, Iveagh Fish Market).

Recent Touring, Ireland:
'This Lime Tree Bower' in association with Fly by Night Theatre Company (1998, Galway, Monaghan, Cork, Castlebar, Letterkenny, Antrim, Armagh).
'The Gay Detective' (1996, Limerick, Cork and Galway).
'Come Good Rain' (1996, Belfast, Limerick, Cork and Galway).

Recent Touring, Overseas:
'The Gay Detective' (1996, Tricycle Theatre, London).

Photo: The new Project Arts Centre.
© Shay Cleary & Associates.

Project Arts Centre

39 East Essex Street
Temple Bar
Dublin 2
Tel: 01 6796622
Fax: 01 6627855
E-mail: info@project.ie
Website: http://www.project.ie

Admin contact: Tom Coughlan
Artistic contact: Fiach Mac Conghail

Project Arts Centre produces and co-produces shows on a regular basis and has a history of commissioning work. Writers currently under commission include Marina Carr, Paul Mercier and Gerard Stembridge.

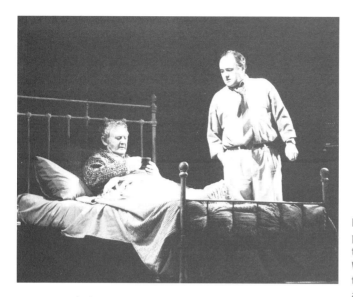

Red Kettle Theatre Company

33 O'Connell Street
Waterford
Tel: 051 879688
Fax: 051 857416
E-mail: rkettle@iol.ie

Admin contact: Liam Rellis
Artistic contact: Jim Nolan

Red Kettle, founded in 1985, is a Waterford based professional theatre company. In addition to productions at its home base, the company tours regularly throughout Ireland and overseas.

Red Kettle is fully committed to create, through its Children's Company, Little Red Kettle, a platform whereby children can participate actively in the theatre process and to make theatre accessible and attractive to young audiences.

Red Kettle's artistic policy is to produce theatre in Waterford, throughout Ireland and where possible overseas. Whilst including work from the existing repertoire, the company specialises in the commissioning and development of new Irish plays for adults and children.

Recent Productions:
'The Salvage Shop' by Jim Nolan.
'Choke My Heart' by Celia McBride.
'The Stomping Ground' by Loughlin Deegan.
'Kyello Oraku and Pearl's Colour Dream' by Ben Hennessy & Liam Meagher.

Recent Touring, Ireland:
'The Salvage Shop' by Jim Nolan.
'The Stomping Ground' by Loughlin Deegan.
'Catalpa - The Movie' by Donal O'Kelly.

Recent Touring, overseas:
'Catalpa - The Movie' by Donal O'Kelly.

Photo: Niall Tóibín and John Olohan in 'The Salvage Shop' by Jim Nolan. © Eoin Murphy.

Founded in 1988, Replay Productions is dedicated to presenting high quality educational theatre to all education sectors (primary, secondary and special needs) supported by workshops/ resource material for teachers and students. Replay Productions was nominated for a Special Judges Award at the 1997 Irish Times / ESB Theatre Awards for its 'comprehensive approach to Theatre In Education'.

Replay is dedicated to broadening the range of high quality theatre for young people by commissioning and producing new plays and introducing existing international scripts of relevance to its audience.

Recent Productions:
'Sinking' by Gary Mitchell (Autumn 1997). 'The Lost Child' by Mike Kenny (Spring 1998).

Replay Productions

Old Museum Arts Centre
7 College Square North
Belfast BT1 6AR
Tel: 01232 322773
Fax: 01232 322724

Admin contract: Ali FitzGibbon
Artistic contact: Janice Jarvis

Recent Touring:
Replay Productions tours all its work to schools and venues throughout Northern Ireland. Regular public venues include The Playhouse, Derry, the Old Museum Arts Centre, Belfast and the Garage Theatre, Monaghan.

Photo: Sheelagh O'Kane as Paul's mother and Ruairi Conaghan as Paul in 'Sinking' by Gary Mitchell, Autumn 1997. © Jill Jennings.

Ridiculusmus

10F Owen O'Cork Mill
288 Beersbridge Road
Belfast BT5 5DX
Tel: 01232 460630
Fax: 01232 460620
E-mail: ridic@globulnet.co.uk

Admin contact: J. Mercer
Artistic contact: Jon Hough and David Woods

Founded in 1992, Ridiculusmus are a highly portable small scale touring outfit with unique comic style and attitude, using the highest quality performance skills.

The company's artistic policy is to make theatre an unrivalled imaginative and entertaining art-form with performances that are comic, of high quality, relevant and give free rein to the creativity of the artists involved.

Recent Productions:
'The Exhibitionists'.
'Omnium (A user's guide)'.
'Hatterr and Chatteertee'.
'The Third Policeman'.

Recent Touring, Ireland:
'The Exhibitionists'.
'Hatterr and Chattertee'.
'The Third Policeman'.

Recent Touring, Overseas:
'The Exhibitionists':
'Hatterr and Chattertee':
'The Third Policeman':

Photo: John Hough in 'The Exhibitionists' © Martin Muller.

Rough Magic commissions, develops and produces new Irish writing as well as contemporary British and American plays and new interpretations of the classics.

Recent Productions:
'The School For Scandal' by Richard Brinsley Sheridan.
'Mrs. Sweeney' by Paula Meehan.
'Halloween Night' by Declan Hughes.
'Northern Star' by Stewart Parker.

Rough Magic Theatre Company

5/6 South Great Georges Street
Dublin 2
Tel: 01 6719278
Fax: 01 6719301
E-mail: roughmag@iol.ie
Website: http://www.iol.ie/~roughmag

Admin contact: Ciara McGlynn
Artistic contact: Lynne Parker

Rough Magic, one of Ireland's leading theatre companies, was formed in 1984. Since its establishment the company has produced more then 50 critically acclaimed productions and has developed a distinctive style and reputation for excellence.

Recent Touring, Ireland:
'The School For Scandal' (1998, Town Hall Theatre, Galway; Gaiety Theatre, Dublin; Cork Opera House).
'Pentecost' (1996, Limerick; Waterford; Longford; Derry; Galway).
'Danti-Dan' (1996, Galway; Limerick; Cork).

Recent Touring, Overseas:
'Halloween Night' (1997, Donmar Warehouse, London).
'Pentecost' (1996, Brighton Festival; Lyceum, Edinburgh; Donmar Warehouse, London).

Photo: Liz Kuti as Maria, Peter Hanly as Joseph Surface and Ingrid Craigie as Lady Sneerwell in 'The School for Scandal' by Richard Brinsley Sheridan produced by Rough Magic Theatre Company. © Amelia Stein.

Second Age aims to encourage
the participation of the best
calibre of theatre practitioners
in its productions and to
promote an awareness and love
of theatre in the audience.

Recent Productions:
'Romeo and Juliet' by William
Shakespeare (1998, Tivoli
Theatre, Dublin).
'Othello' by William
Shakespeare (1997, Tivoli
Theatre, Dublin).
'The Merchant of Venice' by William
Shakespeare (1997, Tivoli Theatre, Dublin).
'King Lear' by William Shakespeare (1996,
Tivoli Theatre, Dublin).

Second Age Theatre Company

74 Dame Street
Dublin 2
Tel: 01 6798542
Fax: 01 6707926

Admin contact: Laura O'Herlihy
Artistic contact: Bryan O'Donoghue

Second Age was founded to create a
magical experience of theatre for a student
audience, by presenting the school
curriculum plays in innovative, theatrical
and dynamic productions.

Recent Touring, Ireland:
'Romeo and Juliet' (1998, Backstage
Theatre, Longford; Belltable Arts Centre,
Limerick; Hawk's Well Theatre, Sligo; Cork
Opera House; Town Hall Theatre, Galway).
'Othello' (1997, Town Hall Theatre, Galway;
Cork Opera House).
'The Merchant of Venice' (1997, Everyman
Palace Theatre, Cork; Siamsa Tire Theatre,
Tralee; Belltable Arts Centre, Limerick;
Hawk's Well Theatre, Sligo; Town Hall
Theatre, Galway).

Photo: Timothy West in 'King Lear'. © Tom Lawlor.

s u b s i d i s e d

The company has developed an original performance style to meet the needs of pieces whose requirements far exceed the demands of naturalistic theatre.

In January 1998, Storytellers premiered 'When The Wall Came Down' by Renate Ahrens-Kramer. The production was given a multi-media treatment and was accompanied by an exhibition from the Checkpoint Charlie Museum in Berlin, including video recordings of interviews with escapees now resident in Ireland. Storytellers look forward to staging this play in Berlin in 1999. The company also continues with its programme for young people in 1998.

Storytellers Theatre Company

5 Aston Quay
Dublin 2
Tel: 01 6711161
Fax: 01 6711159
E-mail: storytel@indigo.ie

Admin contact: Marie Jones
Artistic contact: Mary Elizabeth Burke-Kennedy

Storytellers was established to put on stage narratives from many literary sources and diverse cultural traditions.

Recent Productions
'Hard Times' a new adaptation by Mary Elizabeth-Burke Kennedy (1998).
'When The Wall Came Down' by Renate Ahrens-Kramer (1998).
'Silas Marner' (1997).
'Wuthering Heights' (1996).

Recent Touring, Ireland:
'Hard Times' (1998, Cork, Limerick, Galway, Sligo, Longford and Coleraine).
'When The Wall Came Down' (1998, Cork, Longford and Enniskillen).
'Silas Marner' (1997, Derry, Kilkenny, Cork, Limerick, Sligo, Tralee and Galway).

Photo: Johnny Murphy as Mr. Steinmann in 'When The Wall Came Down' by Renate Ahrens-Kramer. © Tom Lawlor.

TEAM presentations combine exciting entertainment with thought provoking content. TEAM creates high quality theatre which is committed to an educational purpose, exploring in a non-didactic way ideas, attitudes, situations and experiences of direct relevance to young people.

Recent Productions

'Silly Millie's Storybook' by John McArdle (1998, Primary School Programme).
'Mirad - A Boy From Bosnia' by Ad de Bont (1997, Post-Primary School Programme).
'The Voyage' by Paula Meehan (1997, Primary School Programme).
'Black Ice' by Thomas McLaughlin (1996, Post-Primary School Programme).

Recent Touring, Ireland:

TEAM tours to primary and post-primary schools in Dublin, Donegal, Cavan, Longford, Leitrim, Offaly, Sligo, Monaghan, Meath, Kildare, Wicklow and Westmeath.

Photo: Natalie Stringer and A.J. Kennedy from 'Mirad - A Boy From Bosnia' by Ad de Bont. © Colm Henry.

TEAM Educational Theatre Company

4 Marlborough Place
Dublin 1
Tel: 01 8786108
Fax: 01 8748989
E-mail: team@tinet.ie

Admin contact: Jackie Ryan
Artistic contact: Martin Murphy

TEAM has earned national and international acclaim over the last 23 years by creating and presenting original theatre-in-education programmes in schools.

Theatre Omnibus

Theatre Omnibus
Unit 20
Clare Business Centre
Francis Street
Ennis , Co Clare
Tel: 065 29952
Fax: 065 29952
Admin contact: Anne O'Doherty
Artistic contact: Jean Regan/Bernard
Dowd

Founded in 1981 by Bernard Dowd and Jean Regan, Theatre Omnibus continues to develop experimental community theatre of relevance to modern Ireland. The company bridges the gap between community art and fine art by commissioning new Irish writing and music for theatre with community involvement through workshops and by bringing these plays to communities in their own environment. Within County Clare close links have been established with Macra na Feirme and the Disabled People of Clare.

Recent Productions
'Last Nights Fun' - A play combining written text with sounds.
'Irish Women Adventurers' - Create your own show.
'The Spell Of The Mega Mall' - A multi-media play.

Recent Touring, Ireland
'The Spell of The Mega Mall' (Spring 1998; County Clare, Dublin and Dungannon.) Cross Border Project; Theatre Omnibus / Macra na Feirme / Broadroad Theatre Company. (Co. Armagh and Ennis). 'Sense & Sense of Ability' (Autumn 1998). 'Last Nights Fun' (toured to 18 towns and villages and the Dublin Theatre Festival).

Photo: From L to R: Dermot Hayes, Rebah, Edward Cahill, Jean Regan, Thomas Connole, Declan Considine and Bernard Dowd in 'The Spell Of The Mega Mall'. © John Kelly

Tinderbox Theatre Company

McAvoy House
17a Ormeau Avenue
Belfast BT2 8HD
Tel: 01232 439313
Fax: 01232 329420

Admin contact: Eamon Quinn
Artistic contact: Stephen Wright

Tinderbox was formed in 1988 and is one of the main independent theatre companies in Ireland. Tinderbox is the main producer of new Irish work in Northern Ireland and tours two to three productions annually.

Tinderbox is committed to developing new Irish writing. The company commissions writers, produces the annual April Sundays Festival of Play Readings and also presents important contemporary work by Irish playwrights.

Recent Productions
'Second-Hand Thunder' by Joseph Crilly (May - July 1998).
'Into The Heatland' by John McClelland (January - February 1998).
'Dumped' by Daragh Carville (September - October 1997).
'Language Roulette' by Daragh Carville (February - May 1997).

Recent Touring, Ireland:
'Second-Hand Thunder' by Joseph Crilly.
'Dumped' by Daragh Carville.
'Language Roulette' by Daragh Carville.

Recent Touring, Overseas:
'Language Roulette' by Daragh Carville (Bush Theatre, London; Traverse Theatre, Edinburgh).
'A Bright Light Shining' by David Ashton (Traverse Theatre, Edinburgh).

Photo: Julia Dearden and Des Braiden in 'Into The Heartland'.
© Phil Smyth.

The company's artistic policy involves presenting new work and adaptations, frequently in unusual venues. UTC manages the only full time Music Theatre Training Course in Ireland every summer and an accredited Community Theatre Training Course.

Ulster Theatre Company

54 Drumnaconagher Road
Crossgar
Co Down BT30 9JH
Tel: 01396 830166
Fax: 01396 830166
Mobile: 0421 503240
E-mail: michael.h.poynor@lineone.net

Admin contact: Niall Cranney
Artistic contact: Michael Poynor

Ulster Theatre Company is a peripatetic company presenting new work and adaptations with strong educational links through courses for schools, the community sector and pre-professional training. The company tours and stages the largest musical theatre productions created in Ireland.

Recent Productions:
'Murder in the Cathedral' by T.S. Elliot (November 1998).
'Rockin' Mikado' by Michael Poynor and Mark Dougherty based on the G&S original (August - September 1998).
'Scrooge's Christmas' by Michael Poynor and Mark Dougherty (December 1997 - January 1998).
'A Chorus Line' by Michael Bennett (August/September 1997).

Recent Touring, Ireland:
'A Chorus Line'.
'Oklahoma!'.
'Grease'.

Recent Touring, Overseas:
'Rockin' Mikado' (Belfast, Aberden, Scotland; Manchester, England).

Photo: 'A Chorus Line'. © Christopher Hill Photographic.

Upstate is both an international theatre company and a community drama development organisation. In all its programmes and productions the company fosters: artistic innovation, exemplary professional standards, inclusiveness and hope.

Upstate Theatre Project

(incorporating 'Upstate Live')
1 Fair Street
Drogheda
Co Louth
Tel: 041 9844227
Fax: 041 9844232
E-mail: upstate@tinet.ie

Admin contact: Mary Scally,
Company Manager
Artistic contact: Declan Gorman,
Artistic Director

Recent Productions:
'The Weavers' by Gerhart Hamptmann in a new translation by Declan Gorman (1997). 'Hades' by Declan Gorman devised and developed with several artists and local youth theatres (1998).

Recent Touring, Ireland:
'The Weavers' (1997, Dublin Fringe Festival; Garage Theatre, Monaghan). 'Hades' (1998, Cavan; Dundalk) - in progress. Full production available from January 1999

Recent Touring, Overseas:
No touring to date.
Exchanges and partnerships with Live Theatre and Northern Stage, Newcastle-upon-Tyne which commenced in 1998, following the 1997 Theatre Shop.

Photo: Julie Aspell, Steve McArdle and Yvonne Morgan in 'The Weavers'. © Des Clinton.

Yew Theatre Company

Markievicz House
Pearse Street
Ballina
Co. Mayo
Tel: 096 71238
Fax: 096 71238

Admin contact: Caroline McDonagh
Artistic contact: Pierre Campos

As the only professional theatre company in Mayo, the company uses theatre as a medium through which relevant and engaging issues can be explored e.g. 'Melting Doves' - The E Generation. The company tours nationally on an annual basis.

The company's artistic policy promotes accessible theatre through modern and relevant topics with an emphasis on new Irish writers and Irish premieres. Yew Theatre Company also introduces children to drama through devised shows and workshops.

Recent Productions:
'A Man Called Judas' by Claude Puget & Pierre Bost (1998).
'The Mirrorman' by Brian Way (1997, Irish premiere).
'Melting Doves' by Max Hafler (1997, world premiere).
'A Moving Destiny' by Deirdre Hines (1996, world premiere).

Recent Touring, Ireland:
'A Man Called Judas' (1998, National tour).
'Melting Doves'(1997, national tour).
'A Moving Destiny'(1996, national tour).

Photo: Daniel Coll and Debbie Leading in 'A Man Called Judas'. © Yvette Campos.

ARTS
COUNCIL
of Northern Ireland

'...developing the arts
so that as many
people as possible
can enjoy as many
forms of art as
possible to as high a
standard as possible'

MacNeice House, 77 Malone Road, Belfast BT9 6AQ
Tel: +44 (1232) 385200 Fax: +44 (1232) 661715

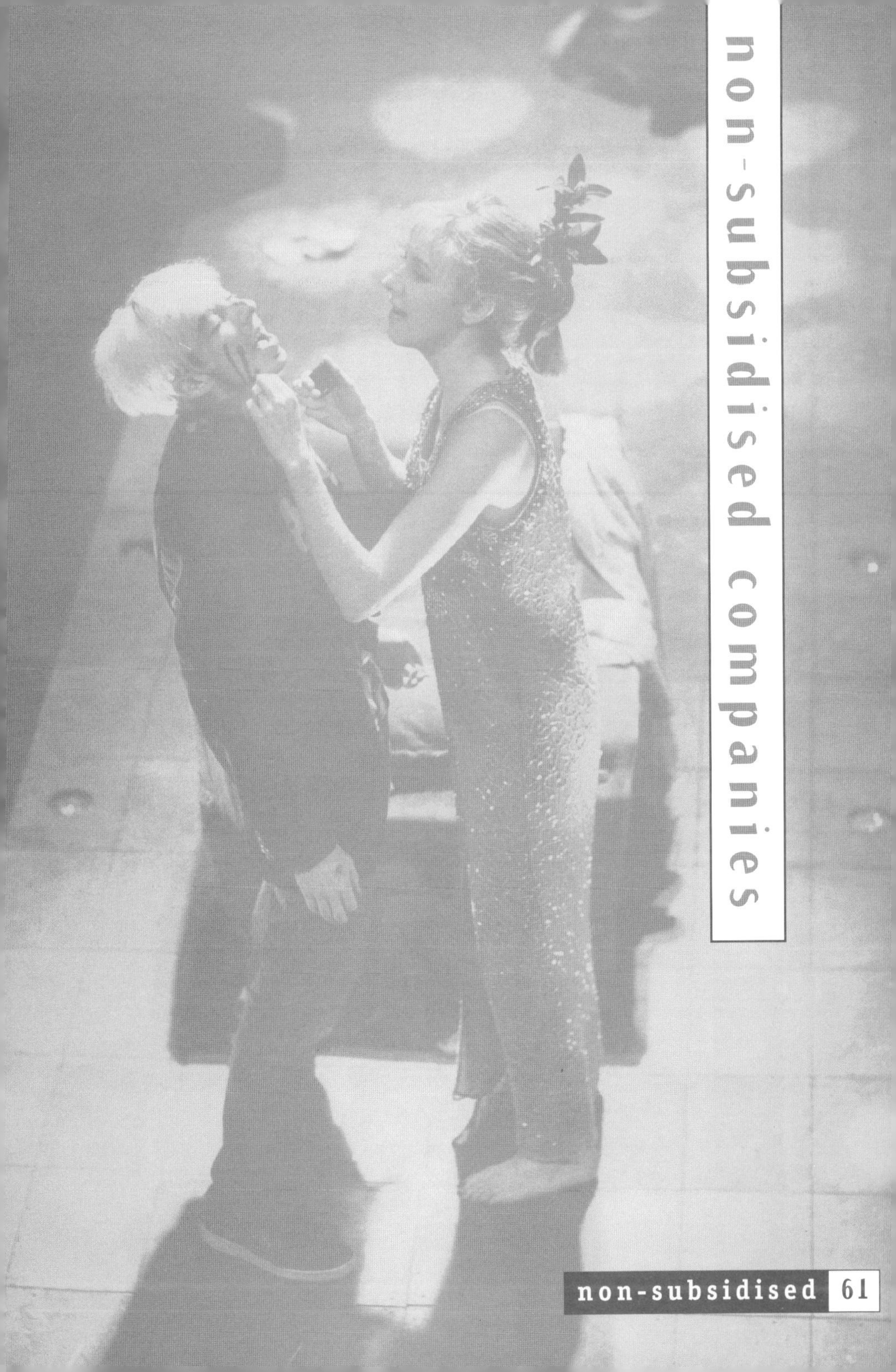

non-subsidised companies

13 spanner company

36 - 37 Lower Ormond Quay, Dublin 1
also:
General Exchagüe 6
Romo (Getxo), Bizkaia, Spain
Tel: 01 8729300
Mobile: 087 635266
Fax: 01 8729478
E-mail: bedrock@clubi.ie
Admin contact: Teresa Lavina
Artistic contact: Ken Harmon.
13 Spanner productions to date - 4 ever
teenage; speed metal farmers; the legend of
me and Voodoo Dolls 'n Double Doves - reflect
the company's primary interests, which are
contemporary alienation, and the point of
intersection between popular culture and the
community. Currently working on a link up
between Dublin and Bilbao.

Ballet Ireland

P.O. Box 5713, Dublin 4
Tel: 0405 57585
Fax: 0405 57585
Artistic contact: Günther Falusy, Anne Maher.
Ballet Ireland, Ireland's new classical ballet
company, has been established to ensure the
performance of the classical repertoire and
new classical works in Ireland by an Irish
company.

Beehive Theatre Company

Kinard West, Lispole
Tralee, Co Kerry, **Tel:** 066 52415
Admin contact: Wendela Rosenberg Polak
Artistic contact: Malcolm George.
From its base in Dingle, Beehive Theatre
Company has been producing challenging and
innovative theatre in West Kerry since 1994.

Beg, Borrow and Steal Theatre Company

35 Leinster Avenue, North Strand, Dublin 3
Tel: 01 8557154
Fax: 01 8557154
Admin/Artistic Contact: Margaret Biggs.
Beg, Borrow and Steal touring theatre in
education company, hosts workshops, bullying
workshops, face painting, parade pageantry,
entertainment and children's parties.
Organisers of Samhain '98 - Dublin's major
Halloween parade.

Black Box Theatre Company

53 South William Street, Dublin 2.
Tel: 01 6799599
Fax: 01 8684032
E-mail: actbox@iol.ie
Contact: Patrick David Nolan.
Black Box are dedicated to new Irish writing
and plays with a relevance to today.

Bloodstone Theatre Company

11 Market Street, Galway
Tel: 091 564747
Admin contact: Lara Campbell
Artistic contact: Denise McNamara.
Bloodstone Theatre Company was founded in
January 1998. The aim of the company is to
produce theatre to the highest standard and
to train its actors, particularly using the
system developed by Constantin Stanislavski.

Boomerang Theatre Company

Teach Barra, Dean Street, Cork
Tel: 021 316826
Fax: 021 316826

E-mail: c/o beardsley@tinet.ie
Admin contact: Ellen Beardsley
Artistic contact: Trish Edelstein.
Boomerang stages more than six professional and youth theatre productions per annum. Its European programme is unparalleled and the company promotes all aspects of contemporary physical theatre.

Brown Penny Theatre Company Ltd

Knockane, Ovens, Co Cork
Tel: 021 331610
E-mail: djryan@tinet.ie
Admin contact: Denis Ryan
Artistic contact: Tim Murphy.
Brown Penny's policy is to produce modern theatre classics in an innovative and exciting format, to develop alternative venues and to allow greater audience access to professional theatre. They also act as a catalyst for new writers bringing their work from page to stage.

Cappucchino Productions

146 Howth Road, Clontarf
Dublin 3
Tel: 01 8336783
Contact: Derby Browne.
Cappuchino Productions presents a collection of music, poetry, drama and dance in a Spanish, Italian and French Bistro style. The company is interested in new settings of established works and also original compositions. Cappuchino Productions consists of harp, guitar, accordion, string quartet and vocals by Derby Browne, plus interesting guests of a mediterranean or kitsch style.

Celtic Mouse Theatre Company

3, St. Barnabas Gardens, Eastwall, Dublin 3
Tel: 01 6676288
Fax: 01 8742869
Admin contact: Jimmy Watson
Artistic contact: Vincent McCabe.
Celtic Mouse produces a range of fresh theatrical harmonies comprised of Irish poetry, literature and song, both contemporary and classical. Productions suitable for theatrical and corporate presentation.

Common Currency Theatre Company

81 Ballybough Road, Dublin 3
Tel: 01 8551332
Artistic contact: Louise Drumm.
Organisers of the Dublin Lorca Festival (Summer '98). The Company explores links between Irish and European theatre, staging plays with European themes / translations of European playwrights. Common Currency also experiment with European staging techniques.

The Connemara Theatre Company Ltd

Doonreaghaun, Cashel, Co Galway
Tel: 095 31049
Fax: 095 31179
Admin contact: Máire Holmes
Artistic contact: Ann Henning Jocelyn.
Based in Connemara, the company specialises in contemporary plays of direct relevance to life in modern society, targeting audiences nationally and internationally whilst pursuing a policy of artistic excellence.

Crooked House Theatre Company

George's Street, Newbridge, Co Kildare
Tel: 045 434297
Mobile: 088 2759420
Fax: 045 435278
E-mail: vtos@tinet.ie
Admin contact: Anna Swords Murphy
Artistic contact: Peter Hussey.
Crooked House emerged from a community theatre collective in the midlands, overseeing ventures such as Kildare Youth Theatre, commissioned theatre, scriptwriting workshops etc. The company premieres new British, Irish and American Theatre.

Echo Echo Dance Theatre Company

The Playhouse
5 - 7 Artillery Street, Derry, BT48 6RG
Tel: 01504 262162
Fax: 01504 262162
Admin contact: Stephen Batts
Artistic contact: Ursula Laeubli.
Professional commissioning company. Small / medium scale. Contemporary / new dance / dance theatre. Teaching / touring Ireland and Europe. Workshops / classes at all levels and ages. Experienced with disability. Playhouse resident company.

Essential Theatre Ensemble Company

The Old Schoolhouse
Loman Street, Trim, Co. Meath
Tel: 01 4542100
Fax: 01 4549686
E-Mail: otuthill@tinet.ie
Admin Contact: Gail Fitzpatrick/Orla Tuthill
Artistic Contact: Neville Carlyle Style.

The Company presents new or recent plays which reflect political/spiritual issues relevant to our times, in a broad range of entertaining theatrical forms. The company has links with companies in South Africa, France, Spain, and the Czech Republic.

Faustroll Productions

7 Manor Place, Stoneybatter, Dublin 7
Tel: 01 6773874 / 8373950
Mobile: 088 2124566
E-mail: faustroll@hotmail.com
Website: http://members.tripod.com/~Faustroll/
Admin contact: Tamsin Young, Julia Carson
Artistic contact: Lynne McCarthy.
Faustroll is a collective dedicated to experimental work, new and neglected writing, and adaptations and translations of foreign works, celebrating the expressive power of theatrical design, music, voice and the body.

Feedback Theatre Company

8 Fitton Street, Morrison's Island, Cork
Tel: 021 277258
Fax: 021 271883
Admin contact: Antoinette Hilliard
Artistic contact: Patrick Talbot.
Feedback presents a mainstream repertoire of classic and contemporary work. Actively co-produces with Everyman Palace Theatre and Triskel Arts Centre. Productions include 'Una Pooka' by Michael Harding, 'Talbots Box' by Thomas Kilroy and Arthur Miller's "A View From The Bridge".

Fly By Night Theatre Company

c/o 22 Daniel Street, Dublin 8
Tel: 01 4539110
Admin contact: Richard Brennan.
Fly by Night's remit is to produce, promote and perform new work for the theatre. Founding members include Richard Brennan, Jason Byrne, Kevin Hely, Conor McPherson, Colin O'Connor. Fly By Night was formed in 1992 and has 12 productions to date.

Flying Pig Comedy Troupe

c/o Town Hall Theatre
Courthouse Square, Galway
Tel: 091 582525
Mobile: 086 8149556
Fax: 091 569664
Admin contact: Sonja Brodie.
The Flying Pigs were conceived in March 1992 to perform lunchtime theatre in Galway 's Kings Head pub. The group devise and perform their own material and the emphasis is on comedy, but has been widened to include street theatre.

Gan Broga Dance Company

c/o Echo Echo, The Playhouse
5 - 7 Artillery Street, Derry BT48 6RG
Tel: 01504 349134
Fax: 01504 262162
Admin & Artistic contact: Ayesha Mailey.
'Semi-professional' dance company in training. Small scale performances of contemporary dance. Animating carnivals and festivals. Teaching and choreography mainly for children under 12 years old. Supported by the Derry Playhouse Education Department.

Giltspur Theatre Company

71 Woodbrook Lawn, Boghall Road
Bray, Co Wicklow
Tel: 01 2867539 **Fax:** 01 2867539
Admin contact: Siobhan Curran
Artistic contact: Lorraine O'Brien.
Giltspur Theatre Company aims to produce new and existing plays, whose themes are relevant to a general audience and feature strong female roles. Giltspur will especially encourage new Irish writing.

Gúna Nua Theatre Company

26 Camden Lock, South Dock Road, Dublin 4
Tel: 01 6608101
Mobile: 087 2377681
Fax: 01 6608101
Admin contact: Éadaoin Glynn
Artistic contact: David Parnell/Paul Meade.
Gúna Nua Theatre Company is committed to using modern styles of theatre to bring a vibrant and dynamic form of storytelling to the stage. The company's first production was 'Four Storeys' written and directed by David Parnell.

Indo-Irish Theatre Combine (I.I.T.C.)

24 Greenmount Road, Terenure, Dublin 6.
Tel: 01 4904734
Fax: 01 4900484
Admin contact: Siraj Zaidi
Artistic contact: Siraj Zaidi.
Indo-Irish Theatre Combine (I.T.T.C.) was formed in 1989 to bring Eastern theatre forms to Ireland.

In Transit Dance Company

20 Belmont Church Road, Belfast BT4 3FF
Tel: 01232 282129
Fax: 01232 282129
Contact: Sandy Cuthbert.
A professional contemporary dance company established in Northern Ireland in 1995 by the Artistic Director Sandy Cuthbert. A young, vibrant company that produces work of a high professional standard, commissioning international dance, whilst positively supporting Irish artists. Supported by the Arts Council of Northern Ireland.

Íomhá Ildánach

Crypt Arts Centre, Dublin Castle, Dublin 2
Tel: 01 6713387
Fax: 01 6713370
E-mail: crypt@clubi.ie
Admin contact: Hugh McGinley
Artistic contact: John O'Brien.
Founded in 1985, Íomhá has produced and co-produced over 40 shows to date, as well as managing The Crypt Arts Centre, Dublin Castle.

Lambert Puppet Theatre

Clifton Lane, Monkstown, Co Dublin
Tel: 01 2800974 / 2801863
Fax: 01 2804772
Website: http://puppet@iol.ie
Admin contact: Miriam Lambert
Artistic contact: Eugene Lambert.
The company operates from a 300 seater theatre in Monkstown offering puppet performances every Saturday with extended runs during Christmas and Easter. School tours run through May and June. Shows are for the very young as well as classic fairytales for children of all ages as well as sophisticated shows for adults. Puppet making workshops. Also museum with extensive antique and exotic puppet collection.

Le Rêve Theatre Project

4 Parkview, Wexford
Tel: 053 45084
Fax: 053 23764 (Wexford Arts Centre)
Contact: Eleanor Feely.
Le Rêve Theatre Project is dedicated to creating stimulating theatre work encompassing visual, aural and sensory imagery together with written texts. It welcomes submissions from artists of all disciplines.

The Little Sisters of Tragedy

12 Leinster Street East, Dublin 3
Tel: 01 855 0843
Contact: Mark Wale.
Physical comedians with conscience. A performers' collective handcrafting new shows that reinvent clowning and commedia traditions. Boundless visual and vocal ingenuity rooted in the performer / audience relationship.

Locus Theatre Company

347 South Circular Road, Dublin 8
Tel: 01 4734702
Contact: Caroline McSweeney.
Locus Theatre Company aims to create the highest standard of new performance theatre. Narrative is resourced directly from the actor and performed in original theatrical forms.

ManDance

Project Arts Centre, 39 East Essex Street Temple Bar, Dublin 2
Tel: 01 6796622
Fax: 01 6627855
E-mail: info@project.ie
Website: http://www.project.ie
Contact: Paul Johnson.
Established in 1991, ManDance presents solo,

duet and group works that theatrically explore contemporary male culture. Project based and project funded by An Chomhairle Ealaíon, ManDance tours nationally and internationally.

Mirage Theatre Company

Kilmurry Church, Monaleen, Co Limerick
Tel: 061 330468
Fax: 061 330468
Admin contact: Joe Carroll
Artistic contact: Joan McGarry.
Mirage Theatre Company produced four plays and toured to over thirty venues, including the Edinburgh Fringe Festival, since its foundation (Oct 1997). It draws from classical and new writing.

Muted Cupid Theatre Company

Outhouse, South William Street, Dublin 2
Tel: 01 4750981
E-Mail: mutedcupid@tinet.ie
Admin contact: James Barry
Artistic Contact: Alan Kinsella.
Muted Cupid is the National Gay and Lesbian Theatre Company. The company's aim is to produce entertaining theatre that has a relevance to the gay community or plays by gay authors. The company also has a community section and hosts regular workshops and small community based theatre projects.

New Balance Dance Company

23 Goatstown Road, Dublin 14
Tel: 01 6605765/2984167
Admin & Artistic contact: Adrienne Brown.
New Balance Dance Company formed in 1987, is committed to excellence and originality in its productions. Over 22 original works have

been created after collaborating with poetry, text and composers.

Pale Mother Theatre Company

40 South Hill, Dartry, Dublin 6
Tel: 086 28175174
Contact: Helen Casey.·
Pale Mother Theatre Company draws on the legacy of Brecht, Piscator and other originators of a political theatre in establishing a voice of dissent. Video footage, slide projectors and live music are all used in the company's productions.

The Read Company

48 Aughavanagh Road, Dublin 12
Tel: 01 4732285
Fax: 01 4732285
Website:
http://www.comedyshack.com/readco
Contact: Michelle Read.
The Read Company was set up in 1996 by actress and comedienne Michelle Read to produce her own work and to pursue other writing and devising which focuses on the female experience particularly through the medium of comedy. 'Romantic Friction' was awarded a Fringe First in the Edinburgh Fringe Festival 1998 and toured nationally in Ireland.

Room B Productions Ltd

"A Doorway to Diversity",
118, Benburb Street Belfast BT12 6JJ
Tel: 01232 580569
E-mail: roomb@compuserve.com
Admin contact: Claire Cogan
Artistic contact: Ann Cunningham.
Room B is a production company whose aim is to produce new alternative theatre. From its beginnings as a Lesbian and Gay Company the decision was made to enlarge its audience-

base by including any theatre which has previously been under-representated within the so-called mainstream.

Rubato Ballet & Community Arts Project

19 Stamer Street, Dublin 8
Tel: 01 4538657
Fax: 01 4784353
E-mail: rubato@iol.ie
Website: http://www.iol.ie/~rubato
Contact: Zelda Quilligan.
Rubato Ballet's artistic policy and aims are to commission Irish choregraphers, designers and composers, as well as presenting first performances of original choreography and music composition. The company has a commitment to live music in performances and dance-in-education workshops and performances. Rubato also embraces the visual arts, collaborating with painters, poets, sculptors and collaborating in theatre, film, community performances and workshops.

Shanakee Productions

7 Chesham Parade, Belfast BT6 8GR
Tel: 01232 806263
Mobile: 0410 541693
Admin contact: Marianne Crossle
Artistic contact: Seamus Fox / Paul McEneaney.
Shanakee has a regional touring remit. New and traditional Irish material is performed in a "Vaudeville" style with a contemporary treatment and features music, magic, comedy and drama.

SHIBBOLETHeatre Company

89 - 91 Academy Street, Belfast BT1 2LS
Tel: 01247 853258
Fax: 01247 853258

E-mail: shib@compuserve.com
Contact: John Mc Ilduff or Emily Mytton.
Based in Belfast, formed in 1997. ShibboleTheatre is committed to original, physical based, international theatre. It has provided two shows 'Floating Babel' (1997) nominated for Belfast City Arts Award and 'The Turnout' (1998) recent Irish tour.

The Sionnach Theatre Company

The New Theatre , 43 East Essex Street
Temple Bar, Dublin 2
Tel: 01 6703361
Fax: 01 6711943
E-mail: sionnach@indigo.ie
Admin contact: Anthony Fox, Leanne Willars, Robert Lane
Artistic contact: Anthony Fox, Robert Lane.
The company is dedicated to the encouragement of young talent and aims to produce plays by Irish authors, focusing on social themes which affect young people today.

Smashing Times Theatre Company Limited

De Valois House, 5 Meetinghouse Lane
off Marys Abbey, Dublin 7
Tel: 01 8727847
Fax: 01 8735537
Contact: Margaret Toomey.
Smashing Times Theatre Company Limited is committed to presenting classical and contemporary plays that explore and celebrate the diversity of women's experiences. The company is committed to exploring new art forms and innovative styles of theatre with a view to challenging the boundaries of what constitutes the female perspective.

Sole Purpose Productions

The Playhouse
5 - 7 Artillary Street
Derry BT48 6RG
Tel: 01504 271126 / 360271
Fax: 01504 261884
Admin contact: Pat Byrne
Artistic contact: Dave Duggan.
Sole Purpose Productions aims to produce theatrical writing and performance to investigate social and public issues. Plays available for touring include 'The Shopper and The Boy' and 'Without The Walls'.

Source Theatre Company

49 Whitechurch Way, Ballyboden, Dublin 16
Tel: 086 8324065
Artistic contact: George Heslin.
Source Theatre Company began by producing Mark O Rowe's first play 'Rundown'. Since then the company has developed work with writers in Dublin and New York. The company will present 'Cooooo Louds' by New York based writer Imelda O' Reilly as part of the Dublin Fringe Festival 1998.

Spotlight Theatre Company

20 Redberry, Finnstown Priory,
Lucan, Co Dublin
Tel: 01 6212373/4936992
Admin contact: Dave Clarke
Artistic contact: Alex McLennan.
Founded in October '96, Spotlight's aim is to produce well-known plays in a "poor theatre" style, as well as plays written within the company.

Tall Tales Theatre Company

25 Glenaulin, Chapelizod, Dublin 20
Tel: 01 6260548
Mobile: 087 2262498
Fax: 01 4573138
Admin contact: Maureen Collender
Artistic contact: Deirdre Kinahan.
Tall Tales provides a forum for new actors, directors and writers. It aims to produce varied, accessible and exciting theatre. The door is always open to new challenges.

The Temenos Project

38 Moyne Road, Ranelagh, Dublin 6
Tel: 01 4960389
Fax: 01 4960389
E-mail: temenos@iol.ie
Admin/Artistic contact: Martin Boroson.
The Temenos Project developes international, performances using transformational techniques (meditation, dreamwork, trance). Currently: Words and I (collaboration with Japanese artists, inspired by the art of Georgia O'Keefe). Studio performance: January 1999, Dublin. World Tour: 2000.

Theatre of Fire

3 Mount Pleasant Villas, Bray, Co Wicklow
Tel: 01 2828273
Mobile: 087 2451644
Fax: 01 2828153
Contact: Maria Hingerty.
Theatre of Fire specialises in creating site specific outdoor theatre for large audiences using fire, fireworks, performance and live music. Site specific work means that the company enjoys the challenge of designing original ideas to suit a given festival both in theme and budget. Theatre of Fire company consists of performers, pyrotechnists, musicians, sculptors, engineers and artists.

The trademarks of the company are Big, Bold, Bright, Colourful, Noisy, Exciting, Surprising, Fun, and of course... Explosive!

Theatre Laboratory

6, Willowmount, Booterstown, Co Dublin
Tel: 088 2179888
Admin contact: Sophie Guillemant
Artistic contact: John Ryan.
The Theatre Laboratory is an experimental company (formed 1990) committed to an improvisational approach to devising productions allowing maximum use of stylised forms linked with text and music.

Three Bags Full Theatre Company

90 Trinity Square, Townsend St., Dublin 2
Tel: 01 6704848
E-mail: antoinetwal@hotmail.com
Contact: Antoinettte Walsh.
Three Bags Full Theatre Company concentrates on creating challenging roles for actors, in particular female roles, as its founding members are all women. The company's recent work has incorporated multi-media such as video, photography and sound to create visually vibrant productions that look at current themes such as xenophobia, racism and gender.

Vesuvius Theatre Company

112 Harolds Cross Road, Dublin 6W
Tel: 01 4962033/4962144
Fax: 01 4962036
Admin contact: Mairéad McCormack
Artistic contact: Vanessa Fielding.
Vesuvius is a young, professional theatre company producing new plays with a social dimension, staged in the Dublin 7 area in alternative and innovative settings,

overcoming the traditional barrier between audience and player.

Who The Hell Theatre Company

63 Ardenvohr Street, Belfast BT6 8NB
Tel: 01232 597483
Admin contact: P.R. Thompson
Artistic contact: Sean Caffrey.
Founded in 1992 to produce plays by living Irish writers. Performing first in Ulster and then touring all of Ireland to small and medium sized community venues.

Will To Swing

19 Percy Lane, Dublin 4
Tel: 01 6687963
Admin contact: Moyra D'Arcy
Artistic contact: Susannah de Wrixon.
A cabaret group that takes material from all areas of music, popular and unknown. Shows include 'A Tribute to Ella Fitzgerald', 'Pyjamajazz', 'An Evening of Brel' and various weddings and parties. It's all a bit of fun!

Yeats Theatre Company

14 Lord Edward Street, Sligo
Tel: 071 46622
Fax: 071 46622
E-mail: yeats@futurenet.ie
Website: http://www.futurenet.ie/yeats
Contact: Edmund Henry.
The company was formed in 1997 for the production and promotion of Yeatsian Drama. The group members have been involved in Yeats plays over a period of twenty five years in association with the Yeats International Summer School.

programming venues

Abymill Theatre

Abbey Street, Fethard,
Co. Tipperary
Tel: 052 31254
Programmer: Austin O'Flynn
Size: 161 seats
Theatre Policy: Available for touring companies, amateur groups and musical societies.

Andrews Lane Theatre

9 - 17 St. Andrews Lane
Dublin 2
Tel: 01 679 5720
Fax: 01 679 7552
Programmer: Pat Moylan
Size: 220 seats (Theatre)
75 seats (studio)
Theatre policy: The theatre's main stage presents mainly professional productions, with a mixture of amateur and professional productions in the studio space upstairs.

Ardhowen Theatre

Dublin Road, Enniskillen
Co Fermanagh BT74 6BR
Tel: 01365 323233 (Admin)
01365 325440 (Box office)
Fax: 01365 327102
Programmer: Eamonn Bradley
Size: 290 seats - Theatre By The Lakes;
100 seats - Gallery Bar;
50 seats - Studio
Theatre Policy: Professional drama, classical music, opera, ballet, dance, blues, jazz, traditional, variety and children's events plus amateur performances and community events.

The Ark, A Cultural Centre for Children

Eustace Street,
Temple Bar, Dublin 2
Tel: 01 6707788
Fax: 01 6707758
E-mail: info@ark.ie
Website: http://www.ark.ie
Programmer: Martin Drury
Size: 150 seats
Theatre Policy: The Ark is principally a producing house presenting its own productions of original theatre and music theatre for children. Occasionally a receiving venue.

Backstage Theatre & Centre for the Arts

Farneyhoogan, Longford
Tel: 043 47889 (Admin)
043 47888 (Box office)
Fax: 043 47890
E-mail: backstage@tinet.ie
Programmer: Jane Hughes
Size: 212 seats
Theatre Policy: Open all year. Receiving house only. Programming mainly drama but covers all disciplines. Willing to host premieres. Particularly interested in drama/dance productions aimed at audience aged 17-25.

Balor Theatre

Main Street, Ballybofey
Co Donegal
Tel: 074 31840
Fax: 074 31840

Programmer: Kieran Quinn, Ben Duffy
Size: 162 seats
Theatre Policy: Theatre companies presented by the Donegal Arts officer Trialach O'Fionnann (See 'Arts Officers').

Bardic Theatre

Donaghmore, Co Tyrone
Tel: 01868 723883 Mgment;
01868 767556 Stage Door
Fax: 01868 724604
Programmer: Sean Faloon
Size: 200 - 220 seats
Theatre Policy: Community theatre serving the mid Ulster area. Also hosting profess-ional theatre companies in partnership with Dungannon District Council.

Bawnacre Centre

Irvinestown
Co Fermanagh BT94 1EE
Tel: 013656 21177
Fax: 013656 28082
Programmer: George Beacom
Size: 300 & 900 seats
Theatre Policy: Hosts and organises a wide variety of entertainment for all age and interest groups including concerts, workshops, drama, dances, exhibitions etc.

Belfast Civic Arts Theatre

23/41 Botanic Avenue
Belfast BT4 1JA
Tel: 01232 316901
Fax: 01232 316906
Programmer: Anthony Stott
Size: 549 seats
Theatre Policy: Theatre's

objectives are to provide a varied programme that will appeal to as many sections of the community as possible.

Belltable Arts Centre
69 O'Connell Street, Limerick
Tel: 061 319709 / 319866
Fax: 061 418552
E-mail: belltabl@iol.ie
Website:
http://www.commerce.ie/bell table
Programmer: Mary Coll
Size: 257 seats
Theatre Policy: To present the best productions available on tour, to encourage tours by companies from Ireland and the U.K., to stimulate audiences for new writing, to keep pushing back the boundaries.

Black Box
Courthouse Square, Galway
Tel: 091 569755
Fax: 091 569664
E-mail: tht@tinet.ie
Website:
http://homepage.tinet.ie/~tht
Programmer: Michael Diskin
Size: 200 - 600 seats
Theatre Policy: Aim is to be at the centre of the arts/ entertainment life of Galway.

Bt Studio
Belfast Waterfront Hall
2 Lanyon Pl., Belfast BT1 3LP
Tel: 01232 334400
Fax: 01232 249862
E-mail:
HusbandsT@waterfront.co.uk

Programmer: Tim Husbands
Size: 264/321/or 482 seats depending on stage configuration
Theatre Policy: The venue promotes a policy of partnership with both home based and visiting companies, including internationally renowned groups.

City Arts Centre
23-25 Moss Street, Dublin 2
Tel: 01 6770643
Fax: 01 6770131
E-mail:
cityartscentre@tinet.ie
Web:
http://homepage.tinet.ie~cit yarts/
Programmer: Collette Farrell
Size: 100 seats
Theatre Policy: City Arts Centre venue operates a busy year long programme with particular focus on community, youth, disability and independent theatre.

Clotworthy Arts Centre
Antrim Castle Gardens
Randalstown Road
Antrim BT41 4LH
Tel: 01849 428000
Fax: 01849 460360
Programmer: Mairin Murray
Size: 96 seats
Theatre Policy: Aims to show innovative yet accessible productions from Northern Ireland and further afield.

Cork Opera House
Emmet Place, Cork
Tel: 021 274308 Admin;
021 270022 Box Office
Fax: 021 276357
E-mail:
operahousecork@tinet.ie
Programmer: Gerry Barnes, Executive Director
Size: 1000 seats
Theatre Policy: A wide variety to a very high standard both professional and amateur. Includes: dance, opera, musicals, drama, comedy and concerts.

Crescent Arts Centre
2 - 4 University Road
Belfast BT7 1NH
Tel: 01232 242338
Fax: 01232 246748
E-mail: cac@dnet.co.uk
Programmer: Louise Emerson
Size: 250 seats
Theatre Policy: The space can be hired for productions. Venue assists with distribution of publicity, promotion and ticket sales.

Crypt Arts Centre
Dublin Castle, Dublin 2
Tel: 01 6713387
Fax: 01 6713370
E-Mail: crypt@clubi.ie
Programmer: Hugh McGinley
Size: 80 seats
Theatre Policy: The Crypt space has a maximum capacity of 80 seats, front of house and box office. New sound system, gallery lights, mobile lighting rig and coffee shop.

Down Civic Arts Centre

2-6 Irish Street, Downpatrick, Co Down BT30 6BN
Tel: 01396 615283
Fax: 01396 616621
Programmer: Veronica Rice
Size: 200 seats

Draíocht

c/o Deanstown House
Main Street, Blanchardstown
Dublin 15
Tel: 01 8209550
Fax: 01 8209551
E-mail: blancpar@iol.ie
Programmer:
Aileen Lebrocquy
Size: 250/600 seats depending on configuration. Also 2,000 (outdoor area), 80 (studio)
Theatre Policy: Receiving house. Opening in 2000. Rents, splits, fees. Mixing all performance disciplines. Local, national and international.

Everyman Palace Theatre

15 MacCurtain Street, Cork
Tel: 021 503077/501673
Fax: 021 502820
Programmer: Geoff Gould, Artistic Director
Size: 628 seats
Theatre Policy: The provision of top quality drama and performance for Cork audiences and the development of Cork's theatrical talents in all its formats.

Firkin Crane

Shandon, Co Cork
Tel: 021 507487
Fax: 021 501124
Programmer:
Mary Brady, Artistic Director
Size: 240 seats
Theatre Policy: Ireland's only dedicated dance venue presents its New Works Series and Solo Independents by invitation. Also a venue for national and international touring dance companies.

Friars' Gate

Sarsfield Street, Kilmallock, Co Limerick
Tel: 063 98727
Fax: 063 20180
Programmer: John Brazill
Size: 130 seats
Theatre Policy: To present a variety of shows by touring companies at least twice each month. Mainly theatrical, also music and dance.

Gaiety Theatre

South King Street, Dublin 2
Tel: 01 6795622
Fax: 01 6771921
Programmer: John Costigan
Size: 1166 seats
Theatre Policy: Mixed Commercial: Musical, Drama, Panto, Opera, Ballet and Comedy.

Galway Arts Centre (Nuns Island Theatre)

47 Dominick Street, Galway
Tel: 091 565886
Fax: 091 568642
Email: gac@indigo.ie
Programmer: Paul Fahy
Size: 110 (Nuns Island), 50 (#47).
Theatre policy: Touring venue. All productions considered. Rentals/box office percentages.

Garage Theatre

Mifet Complex, Armagh Road
Monaghan
Tel: 047 81597
Fax: 047 81564
Programmer:
Genevieve Gallagher
Size: 160
Theatre policy: A local community theatre venue for both professional touring theatre from Ireland and overseas and for amateur groups to perform in. Provision for young people in theatre/workshops.

Garter Lane Arts Centre

22a O'Connell St., Waterford
Tel: 051 877153
Fax: 051 871570
E-mail: admin@garterlane.ie
Programmer: Lilly O'Reilly
Size: Up to 250 seats
Theatre Policy: Presenting the best of local, national and international work, primarily serving the local and regional audience.

Gorey Little Theatre

Pearse Street,
Gorey, Co Wexford
Tel: 055 21474
Programmer: Dennis Howell
Size: 330 seats
Theatre Policy: Promoting dance and drama.

Grand Opera House

Great Victoria Street
Belfast, BT2 7HR
Tel: 01232 240411
Fax: 01232 236842
E-mail:
dnicholls@gohbelfast.com
Website:
http://www.gohbelfast.com
Programmer: Derek Nicholls
Size: 1001 seats
Theatre Policy: No 1 touring theatre - mixed programme: Ballet/Dance, Opera; Musicals; Children's/Family shows; Comedy; Concerts; Amateur Productions; Education; Entertainment.

The Half Moon Theatre

Cork Opera House
Emmet Place
Cork
Tel: 021 274308
Fax: 021 276357
Programmer: Gerry Barnes
Size: 150 (seated), 250 (standing)
Theatre Policy: Late night music, comedy and drama.

Harmony Hill Arts Centre

54 Harmony Hill
Lisburn BT27 4ES
Tel: 01846 678219
Fax: 01846 662679
Programmer: Siobhán Stewart, Arts Development Officer
Theatre Policy: To mount and present a balanced programme of professional and amateur performing arts activities for local residents and visitors from further afield.

Hawk's Well Theatre

Temple Street, Sligo
Tel: 071 61526
Fax: 071 71737
E-mail: hawkswell@tinet.ie
Website:
http://homepage.tinet.ie/~hwt
Programmer: Denis Clifford, Executive Director
Size: 350 seats
Theatre Policy: To present a range of quality accessible arts events to the widest possible audience in our community, the North West region and for our visitors.

The Mall Theatre & Cinema

Stable Lane, Tuam, Co Galway
Tel: 093 25166
Fax: 093 24463
Programmer:
Jarlath P. Canney
Size: 215 seats
Theatre Policy: Promotion of

live theatre in conjunction with utilising the venue for cinema.

Old Museum Arts Centre

7 College Square North
Belfast BT1 6AR
Tel: 01232 235053
Fax: 01232 322912
Programmer: Elaine Gaston
Size: 90 seats
Theatre Policy: To present the best of new Irish and International theatre, dance, music, poetry and visual arts in the heart of Belfast.

Olympia Theatre

72 Dame Street, Dublin 2
Tel: 01 6777744
Fax: 01 6799474
Programmer: Gerry Sinnott
Size: 1300 seats
Theatre Policy: Receiving theatre for plays, musicals, opera, ballet and music concerts. Midnight concerts every Friday and Saturday.

Players Theatre

Samuel Beckett Centre
Trinity College, Dublin 2
Tel: 01 7022351
Fax: 01 6778996
Programmer: Students Union
Size: 90 seats
Theatre Policy: Venue run by Trinity Players Drama Group. Occasionally available for outside companies.

Project Arts Centre

39 East Essex Street
Temple Bar, Dublin 2
Tel: 01 6796622 (Admin)

1850 260027 (Info /Booking)
Fax: 01 6627855
E-mail: info@project.ie
Website:
http//:www.project.ie
Programmer:
Fiach MacConghail
Size: Temporary venue, project @ the mint, has 120 seats. The new building, due for completion in late 1999, will house two multi-configurable spaces with 220 - 250 seats and 100 seats respectively
Theatre Policy: To encourage and foster emerging and established artists in the creation of new and innovative work.

Riada Centre

33 Garryduff Road
Ballymoney , Co Antrim
Tel: 012656 65792
Fax: 012656 63592
Programmer: Paul Lyness, Recreation Manager
Size: 500 seats
Theatre Policy: Community Programming for adults and children.

Rialto Entertainment Centre

5 Market Street
Derry BT48 6EF
Tel: 01504 264177
Fax: 01504 260688
Website: http://www.mni.co.uk/see/derry/festival
Programmer:
David McLaughlin
Size: 960+ seats
Theatre Policy: Touring plays

and musicals, ballet, dance, concerts (rock, popular and classical), children's entertainment, one-night stands, community theatre and amateur productions.

Riverside Theatre

University of Ulster
Cromore Road
Coleraine
Co. Londonderry BT52 1SA
Tel: 01265 324683
Fax: 01265 324924
Programmer: Janet Mackle
Size: 274 (proscenium), 358 (thrust)
Theatre policy: The venue presents small to middle scale touring drama (classics, contemporary, international, Irish and new works), ballet, contemporary dance, musicals, opera, contemporary music and an annual Christmas show.

Samuel Beckett Centre

Trinity College, Dublin 2
Tel: 01 6081334
Fax: 01 6793488
Web:
http://www.tcd.ie/Drama
Programmer: Richard Seager
Size: 208 seats

Siamsa Tíre Theatre

Town Park, Tralee, Co Kerry
Tel: 066 7123055
Fax: 066 7127276
Programmer: Martin Whelan
Size: 355 seats
Theatre Policy: Folk theatre; Professional and amateur

theatre; Music - classical, traditional and jazz; Dance; Literary events; Opera.

St. Johns Arts Centre

The Square, Listowel, Co Kerry
Tel: 068 22566
Fax: 068 23485
Website: http://www/kerry-web.ie/destinationkerry/listowel/squarehtml.
Programmer: Joe Murphy
Size: 134 seats
Theatre Policy: Local, national and international productions and co-productions; Youth theatre projects.

St. Michaels Theatre

South Street, New Ross
Co Wexford
Tel: 051 421255
Fax: 051 420346
Programmer:
Mrs. Helen Lewis, Manager
Size: 329 seats
Theatre policy: To promote professional and amateur local, national and international productions in all aspects of music, drama, dance and exhibitions.

Taibhdhearc nc Gaillimhe

An tSráid Láir, Gaillimh
Tel: 091 562024 / 563600
Fax: 091 563195
E-mail: taibh@iol.ie
Programmer: Aoife Ní Scolaí
Size: 180 seats
Theatre Policy: Taibhdhearc

na Gaillimhe is the national theatre of the Irish language. Productions welcome in all languages with priority given to Irish language productions. Also, rehearsal space available which is suitable for workshops, auditions, meetings etc.

Theatre Royal

High Street, Wexford
Tel: 053 22400 (Admin)
Fax: 053 24289
E-mail: info@wexopera.iol.ie
Website:
http://www.iol.ie/~wexopera
Programmer: Jerome Hynes
Size: 550 seats
Theatre Policy: The Theatre Royal acts primarily as the home of Wexford Festival Opera but is keen to have touring productions play Wexford. By virtue of funding the theatre is available on a rental basis only.

Tivoli Theatre

135-138 Francis Street
Dublin 8
Tel: 01 4546367 (Admin)
01 4544472 (Box office)
Fax: 01 4533167
Programmer:
Tony Byrne/Doug Murray
Size: 500 seater theatre;
960 Cabaret/Performance/
Rock area
Theatre policy: A commercial venue presenting various theatre, dance and music events.

Town Hall Theatre

Courthouse Square, Galway
Tel: 091 569755
Fax: 091 569664
E-mail: tht@tinet.ie
Website:
http://homepage.tinet.ie/~tht
Programmer: Michael Diskin
Size: 393
Theatre Policy: Aim is to be at the centre of the arts/ entertainment life of Galway.

The Tyrone Guthrie Centre

Annaghmakerrig
Newbliss, Co. Monaghan
Tel: 047 54003
Fax: 047 54380
E-mail: thetgc@indigo.ie
Programmers:
Bernard Loughlin, Director;
Grainne Millar, Projects Manager
Size of venue: 100
Theatre Policy: The Tyrone Guthrie Centre offers a large rehearsal and performance space for small scale dance, theatre and music performances and collaborations throughout the year.

UCC Granary Theatre

Mardyke
Cork
Tel: 021 904272 / 906275
Fax: 021 904272
E-mail:
info@uccgranary.iol.ie
Programmer:
Granary Committee
Size: 210

Theatre policy: UCC Granary Theatre (opened 1995) is a purpose-built facility located just off campus, on the Mardyke. The building offers teaching, rehearsal and performance space, and is one of the busiest centres in UCC. A lively tradition of student work continues to flourish in Cork, and seasons run from autumn to late spring each year.

Watergate Theatre

Parliament Street, Kilkenny
Tel: 056 61674
Fax: 056 51780
Programmer: Gerry Cody
Size: 328 seats
Theatre Policy: Dealing mainly in theatre, dance, opera and comedy. The theatre is open to guarantee/rental agreements with companies.

Wexford Arts Centre

Cornmarket, Co Wexford
Tel: 053 23764
Fax: 053 24544
Programmer: Denis Collins
Size: 122 seats
Theatre Policy: To present a wide range of small scale theatre in a diversity of styles by local/visiting amateur/professional companies.

Artistes Representatives

29/30 Dame Street
Dublin 2
Tel: 679 8401 Fax: 679 8353

Shall We Dance?

A comprehensive report on
Vocational Dance Training in Ireland
by Anna Leatherdale and Victoria Todd

is now available free of charge from

The Arts Council / An Chomhairle Ealaíon
70 Merrion Square
Dublin 2
Ireland
Tel + 353 1 618 0200
Fax + 353 1 661 0349 / 676 1302

The Arts Council
An Chomhairle Ealaíon

Shall We Dance? is a publication of
The Arts Council/An Chomhairle Ealaíon
and The Arts Council of Northern Ireland

festivals

Baboró Festival For Young People

The Black Box, Dyke Road, Galway
Tel: 091 562594
Fax: 091 562655
E-mail: gaf@iol.ie
Programming Director: Jean Parkinson
Theatre Policy: Ireland's only multidisciplinary arts festival for children and young people. It includes an extensive international theatre programme with a full selection of supporting workshops and school visits.
Festival dates:
13 - 18 October 1998;
14 - 19 October 1999.

Belfast Festival at Queen's

Festival House
25 College Gardens
Belfast BT9 6BS
Tel: 01232 667687
Fax: 01232 663733
E-mail: festival@qub.ac.uk
Website: http://www.qub.ac.uk/festival
Programmer:
Sean Doran 1998
Robert Agnew (Executive Director)
Theatre Policy: Presents the best of international and indigenous performing and visual arts for local and visiting audiences.
Festival dates: 12 - 29 November 1988;
29 October - 14 November 1999.

Belfast Fringe Festival

25 College Gardens
Belfast BT9 6BS
Tel: 01232 660515
Fax: 01232 663733
E-mail: c.mcavinchey@qub.ac.uk
Programming Director: Caoimhe McAvinchey
Theatre Policy: The Belfast Festival Fringe is open to everyone, amateur or professional, across all disciplines, from anywhere in the world.
Festival dates:
10 - 28 November 1998;
29 Oct. - Nov. 14 1999

Clifden Community Arts Week

Clifden, Co Galway
Tel: 095 21164 / 21295
Fax: 095 21481
E-mail: artsweek@mouse.ie
Programming Director: Brendan Flynn
Theatre Policy: To bring the best from all of the creative arts to the community with a very strong emphasis on the arts in education.
Festival dates: Sept. 23rd - October 3rd 1999

Dublin Fringe Festival

36/37 Lower Ormond Quay, Dublin 1
Tel: 01 8729016
Fax: 01 8729138
E-mail: fringe@tinet.ie

Website:
http://www.fringefest.com
Programming Director: Ali Curran
Theatre Policy: The DFF programmes theatre, dance and performing art from Irish and international companies. Specific areas of focus are new Irish writing and work not previously produced in Ireland, innovative production style, physical theatre, and work from young recently formed companies.
Festival dates: Monday 28th September - Saturday 17th October 1998.

Dublin Theatre Festival

47 Nassau Street, Dublin 2
Tel: 01 6778439
Fax: 01 6797709
E-mail: dubfest@iol.ie
Web:
http://www.iftn.ie/dublinfestival
Programming Director: Tony Ó Dalaigh & Fergus Linehan
Theatre Policy: The Festival programmes 20 productions, half Irish and half visiting and a season of 3 - 6 children's productions.
Festival dates: 4 - 16 October 1999.

Eigse Carlow Arts Festival

Bridewell Lane, Carlow
Tel: 0503 40491
Fax: 0503 40491
Programming Director: Paddy McGovern
Theatre Policy: Our policy is to cater for children and adult audiences - providing a choice of plays in English and 'as Gaeilge'.

Galway Arts Festival

The Black Box, Dyke Road, Galway
Tel: 091 562594
Fax: 091 562655
E-mail: gaf@iol.ie
Programming Director: Ted Turton
Theatre Policy: Programme includes an extensive, eclectic and innovative international theatre programme featuring major Irish, European and world premieres.
Festival dates: 12 - 25 July 1999.

International Puppet Festival Ireland

Clifton Lane, Monkstown, Co Dublin
Tel: 01 2800974 / 2801863
Fax: 01 2804772
E-mail: puppet@iol.ie
Programming Director: Miriam Lambert
Theatre Policy: An annual puppet festival, now in it's sixth year, featuring puppeteers from all over the world. Thirty one countries have been represented over the past six years bringing great cultural diversity and different puppet styles to Irish audiences. Performances are for adults and children with local library and school performances as well as open air family days.
Festival dates: 10 - 19 September 1998.

Sligo Arts Festival

Model Arts Centre, The Mall, Sligo
Tel: 071 69802
Fax: 071 69802
Programming Director: Danny Kirrane
Theatre Policy: Sligo Arts Festival presents a minimum of two "brought in" theatre productions and encourages local theatre groups to participate in the festival.
Festival dates: 28 May - 7 June 1999.

St. Patrick's Festival

St. Stephen's Green House Earlsfort Terrace, Dublin 2
Tel: 01 676 3205
Fax: 01 676 3208
E-mail: info@paddyfest.ie
Programming Director: Rupert Murray
Theatre Policy: A national celebration of professionally led street theatre, with heavy and diverse community involvement. Free and open for all to enjoy.
Festival dates: 13 - 17 March 1999

Waterford Spraoi

The Glen, Waterford
Tel: 051 841808
Fax: 051 858023
E-mail: spraoi@tinet.ie
Website: http://www.voyager.ie/spraoi '99/index.htm
Programming Director: Miriam Dunne
Theatre Policy: Specialist street theatre/performance/rhythm festival with strong international content.
Festival dates: 30th July - 1st August 1999.

Westport Arts Festival

c/o Resource Centre Mill Street, Westport, Co Mayo
Tel: 098 26787
Fax: 098 26787
Programming Director: Sinéad Wall
Theatre Policy: This is a ten day celebration of the arts including dance, drama, music of all kinds and workshops.
Festival dates: 17 - 26 September 1998.

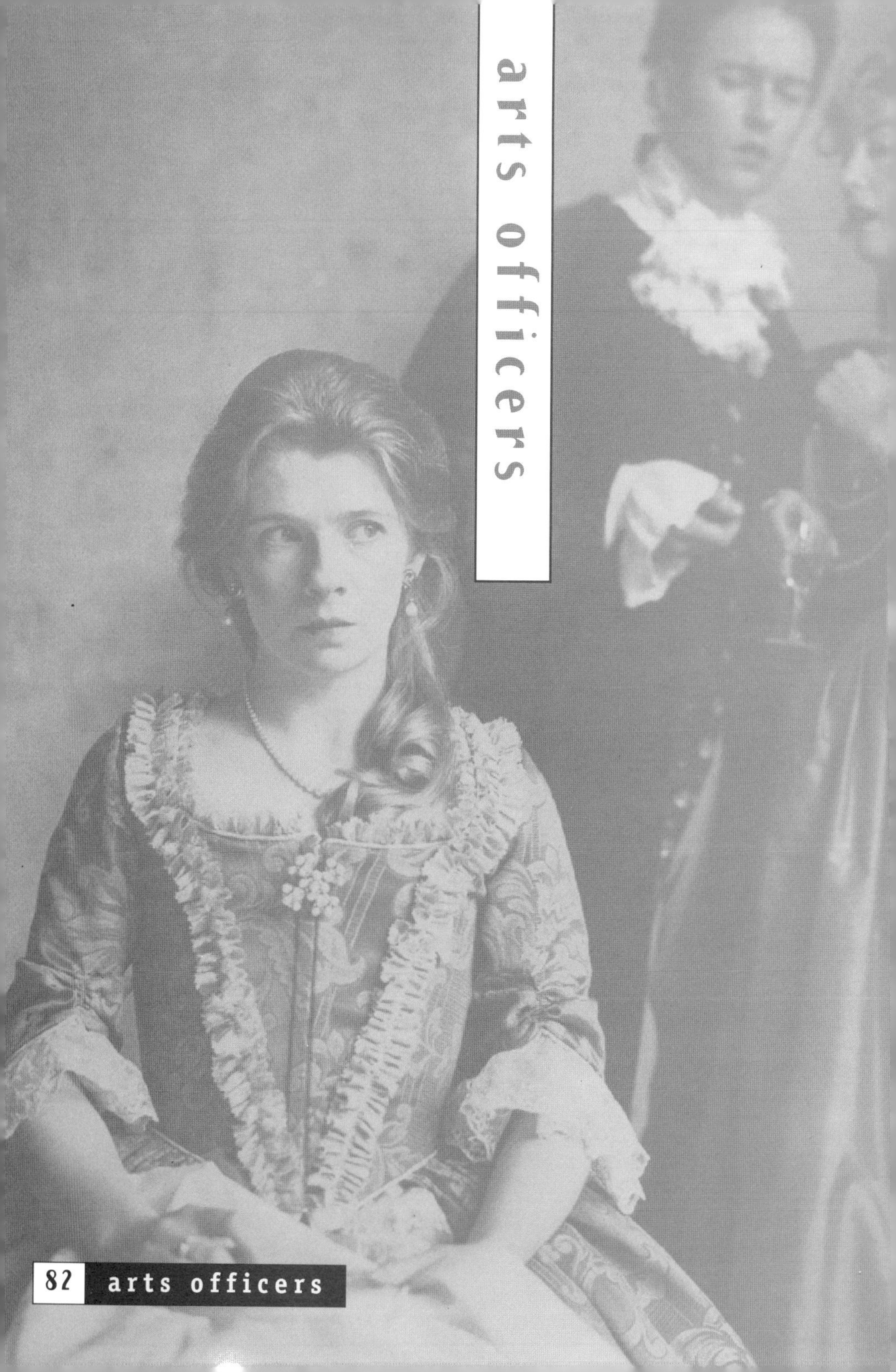

arts officers

Republic of Ireland Arts Officers

Cavan County Council
Ms. Catriona O'Reilly
Tel: (049) 31799

Clare County Council
Mr. Noel Crowley
Tel: (065) 21616

Cork Corporation
Mr. Mark Mulqueen
Tel: (021) 966222

Cork County Library
Mr. Ian McDonagh
Tel: (021) 346210

Donegal County Library
Mr. Traolach Ó Fionnáin
Tel: (074) 21968

Dublin Corporation
Mr. Jack Gilligan
Tel: (01) 8722816

Dundalk UDC
Mr. Brian Harten
Tel: (042) 32276

Dun Laoghaire Corporation
Ms. Cliodhna Shaffrey
Tel: (01) 2806961

Fingal County Council
Mr. Rory O'Byrne
Tel: (01) 8727777

Galway County Council
Mr. James Harrold
Tel: (091) 567722

Kerry County Library
Mr. Pat Walsh
Tel: (066) 21200

Kildare Co. Library
Ms. Mary Linehan
Tel: (045) 31109

Kilkenny Co. Council
Ms. Margaret Cosgrove
Tel: (056) 52699

Laois County Hall
Ms. Muireann Ní Chonaill
Tel: (0502) 22044

Limerick Corporation
Ms. Sheila Deegan
Tel: (061) 415799

Limerick County Council
Ms. Joan McKernan
Tel: (061) 318477

Longford County Council
Mr. Fergus Kennedy
Tel: (043) 48376

Mayo Library Headquarters
Mr. John Coll
Tel: (094) 24444

Meath County Council
Ms. Gerardette Bailey
Tel: (046) 21581 (ext 274)

Monaghan County Council
Mr. Somhairle MacCoghail
Tel: (047) 82211

Offaly County Council
Ms. Sharon Mee
Tel: (0506) 21419

Roscommon County Library
Ms. Emer Leavy
Tel: (0903) 26100

Sligo County Council
Ms. Mary McAuliffe
Tel: (071) 56629

South Dublin County Council
Ms. Gina Kelly
Tel: (01) 4620000

Waterford Corporation
Mr. Derek Verso
Tel: (051) 873501

Wexford County Council
Ms. Lorraine Comer
Tel: (053) 42211

Wicklow County Council
Ms. Deirdre Enright
Tel: (0404) 20155

Northern Ireland Arts Officers

Antrim Borough Council
Mr. Gary Shaw
Tel: (01849) 428000

Ards Borough Council
Ms. Eilis O'Baoill
Tel: (01247) 810803

Armagh District Council
Ms. Kate Bond
Tel: (01861) 521801

Ballymena Borough Council
Ms. Rosalind Lowry
Tel: (01266) 660300

Belfast City Council
Mr. Chris Bailey
Tel: (01232) 320202

Castlereagh Borough Council
Ms. Janine McMacken
Tel: (01232) 483611

Coleraine Borough Council
Mr. Malcolm Murchison
Tel: (01265) 833959

Cookstown District Council
Ms. Linda McGarvey
Tel: (016487) 62205

Craigavon District Council
Ms. Rosaleen McMullan
Tel: (01762) 341618

Derry City Council
Mr. David McLaughlin
Tel: (01504) 266657

Down District Council
Ms. Jill Holmes
Tel: (01396) 615283

Fermanagh District Council
Mr. Eamonn Bradley
Tel: (01365) 323233

Lisburn Borough Council
Ms. Siobhan Stewart
Tel: (01846) 678219

Newry and Mourne District Council
Mr. Mark Hughes
Tel: (01693) 66232

North Down Borough
Ms. Paula Clamp
Tel: (01247) 270371

Omagh District Council
Ms. Jean Brennan
Tel: (01662) 245321

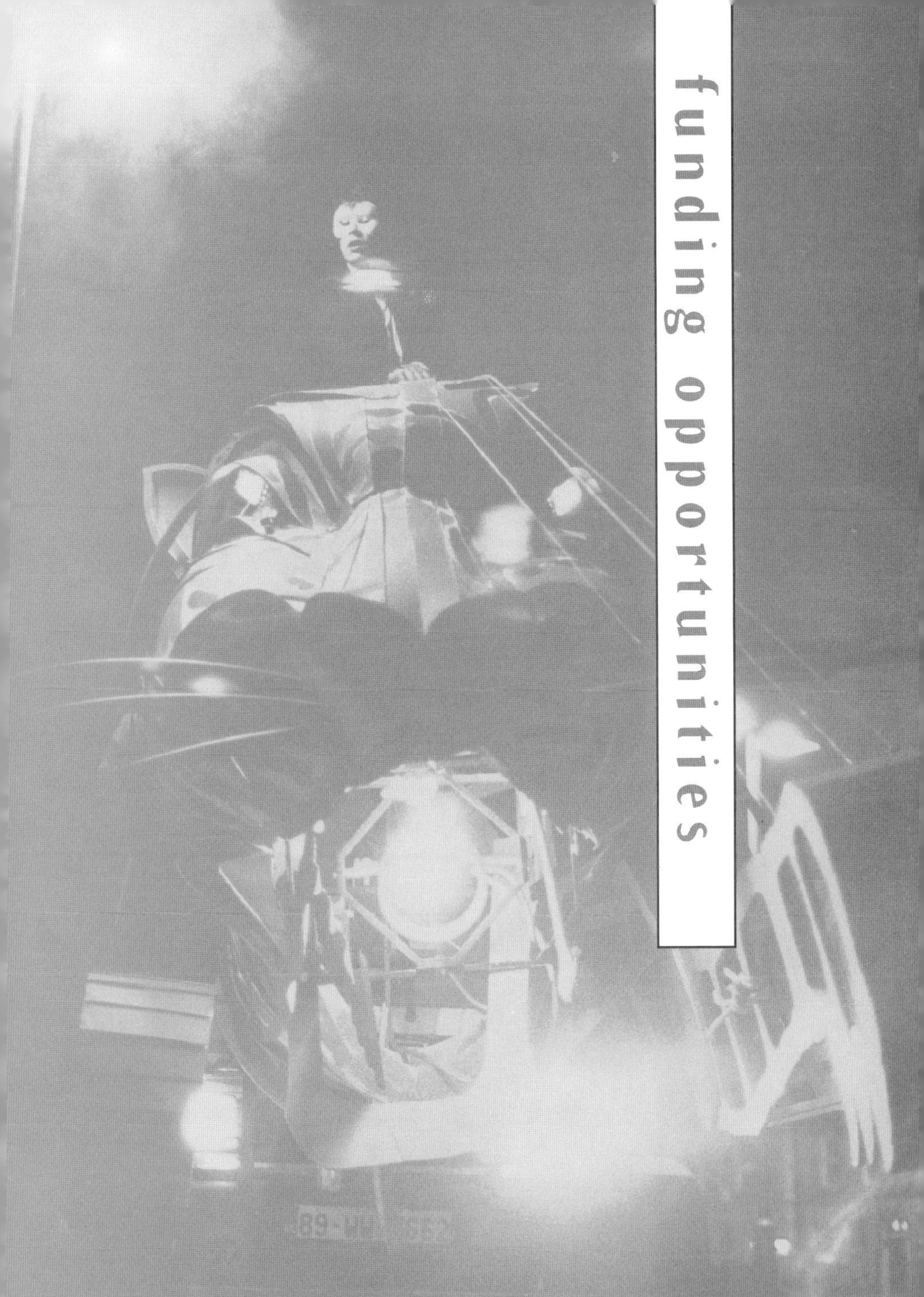

funding opportunities

THE ARTS COUNCIL/AN CHOMHAIRLE EALAÍON

70 Merrion Square, Dublin 2
Tel: 01 6180200
Callsave: 1850 392492
Fax: 01 6610349 / 01 6761302
Contact:
Phelim Donlon, Drama and Opera Officer
Gaye Tanham, Youth Arts and Dance Officer
Tara Byrne, Bursaries Executive

The Arts Council is an independent state body which acts as the development agency for the arts in Ireland; it is the primary source of support for the individual creative and interpretative artist. Its funds come from the Department of Arts, Heritage, Gaeltacht and the Islands. The role of the Arts Council is to provide advice to government on artistic matters, to provide advice, assistance and support to individuals and arts organisations and to a wide range of governmental and non-governmental bodies on arts matters, and to provide financial assistance and other forms of support to individuals and organisations, for artistic purposes.

Funds: The Arts Council provides support to companies and venues throughout the country as well as providing awards and bursaries for the development of individual artists working within the theatre and dance sectors, including administrators (see section 'Funding Available to Individuals'). The areas eligible for support include professional drama, dance and mime, theatre and dance in education, youth theatre, youth and community dance, puppetry and circus. Areas not normally considered include amateur drama groups, charity events, variety artistes and shows and cabaret. Arts Council funding to organisations is denominated in three categories: Revenue Funding, Project Funding and Capital Funding.

Revenue funding: Revenue grants to arts organisations account for 74% of total annual expenditure by the Arts Council. Through its drama and dance budgets the Council provides annual revenue grant assistance to the National Theatre Society and to theatre and dance based production companies throughout the country. It also supports non-theatre-based production companies, theatres, theatre and dance festivals, drama and dance touring, and resource organisations in theatre and dance.

Project Funding: Theatre companies may be offered 'Project' funding on a one-off basis.

Capital funding: The Arts Council allocates a dedicated fund for capital purposes annually. At present, capital funding is distributed over four schemes: Category A - equipment grants; Category B - repairs and refurbishment of existing buildings; Category C - small buildings support; Category D - major proposals.

Other funding: The Arts Council also operates a number of commissioning schemes, including The Arts Centres Commission Scheme, the Inter-Disciplinary Collaborative Commission Scheme, the Dance Commission Scheme and the Playwrights Commission Scheme, which allow organisers and companies to commission and develop new original work in the different disciplines. Dance Project Awards and Drama Mise en Scène Awards are available for one-off projects which encourage innovation and experimentation in dance and drama respectively. The Youth Theatre Project Scheme is a new award which assists various Youth Theatre Projects across the country.

Application procedures: Applications for revenue funding are made using a standard form which is available from The Arts Council.

Applications are considered once a year, the deadline in 1998 being September 30th. Application forms for capital funding are also available. The closing dates in 1998 were as follows: categories A, B and C - 24th April; category D - 28th August. Application procedures for the other funding opportunities vary and information on these is available from the relevant officer at the Arts Council.

Useful publications: General information regarding the Arts Council's activities are outlined in *About the Arts Council*. The criteria and conditions relating to revenue funding are outlined in *Revenue Funding*. *Awards & Opportunities* contains information on support offered to individuals and gives further detail on the other funding opportunities outlined above. All these titles are available from the Arts Council at the above address.

ARTS COUNCIL OF NORTHERN IRELAND

MacNeice House
77 Malone Road, Belfast BT9 6AQ
Tel: 01232 385200
Fax: 01232 661715
Contact: Philip Hammond, Director of Performing Arts; Imelda Foley, Drama and Dance Officer

The Arts Council of Northern Ireland is a statutory body funded by the Department of Education for Northern Ireland. It is the prime distributor of public support for the arts in Northern Ireland. Its mission statement is 'to develop the arts in Northern Ireland so that as many people as possible can enjoy as many forms of art as possible to as high a standard as possible'.

Funds: Theatre and dance organisations are funded through the Department of Performing Arts who list 'the sustaining of the major

performing arts organisations which cater for the preservation of the past, the continuum of the contemporary and the formation of the future' as a priority of the department. Support available to individuals working in the theatre and dance sector is outlined in Awards, Competitions and Bursaries and the Arts Council's National Lottery Fund is outlined in greater detail later in this section.

Revenue funding: Major arts organisations operating all year round and implementing an artistic and financial policy agreed in partnership with the Council receive renewable annual revenue grants. Arts Council awards revenue grants to the following organisations: theatres, theatre companies, festivals, and amateur and youth drama.

Project funding: Four times a year smaller, project-based grants are allocated as a means of supporting individual arts events as they take place during the year.

Application procedure: Standard application forms are available for both Revenue and Project funding applications. Revenue grants are made annually, the deadline for completed applications falls in October of each year. Project grants are made four times annually. It is advisable to check precise deadlines with the Arts Council.

Useful publications: *'Arts Council of Northern Ireland, Information 1989'* available from the above address.

ARTS COUNCIL OF NORTHERN IRELAND NATIONAL LOTTERY FUND

The Lottery Department
Arts Council of Northern Ireland,
MacNeice House
77 Malone Road, Belfast BT9 6AQ
Tel: 01232 667000
Fax: 01232 664766
Contact: Tanya Greenfield, Director

The Arts Council of Northern Ireland has responsibility for distributing lottery funds to the arts in Northern Ireland. The principal aim of lottery funding is to achieve the maximum benefit for the general public through support for arts projects which make an important and lasting difference to the quality of life. The funds are administered by the National Lottery Department which has its own staff reporting directly to the Board of the Council.

Funds: Funding is normally only available for capital expenditure e.g. new buildings, building refurbishment, major items of equipment. Funds are also available, however, for commissioning new work in all art forms and to assist young people undertaking professional training at colleges and institutions in England. 'Access to the Arts' allows lottery funding to be spent on time-limited revenue projects while 'Advancement' will allow arts organisations to plan for a sustainable future.

Application procedure: A detailed application pack is available from the above address. Applications are accepted all year round and are considered on a rolling basis.

Useful publications: *'The Arts Council of Northern Ireland, The National Lottery Arts Fund'* outlines details of the department's arts funding activities. The department also publishes a newsletter entitled *'Arts Lot'* which contains up to date information on lottery funding decisions.

THE BRITISH COUNCIL

22-24 Lower Mount Street, Dublin 4
Tel: 01 6764088
Fax: 01 6766945
Contact: Harold Fish, Director

The British Council, whose aim in Ireland is to promote Anglo-Irish relations through cultural and educational co-operation, opened an office in Dublin in 1990. The council's primary brief within bi-lateral relations is to support those Irish institutions that seek to bring to Ireland British cultural events or explore the possibility of co-productions with cultural organisations in Britain.

Funds: The Council's main area of assistance is in the form of travel grants towards the cost of an air fare to enable artists to travel between Ireland and Britain for cultural events/workshops. Limited funding for other costs may also be available, at the discretion of the director.

Application Procedure: No formal application form exists. Applications should be made in writing at least six weeks before the project's commencement date. Applications should include background information on the organisations and individuals involved, as well as specific information and costings regarding the event to be funded.

THE BRITISH COUNCIL IN NORTHERN IRELAND

1 Chlorine Gardens, Belfast BT9 5DJ
Tel: 01232 666770/01232 666706
Fax: 01232 665242
E-mail: peter.lyner@britcoun.org.uk
Contact: Peter Lyner, Director

The British Council in Northern Ireland aims to ensure that the region's unique expertise and experience are known and exploited in pursuit of the Council's corporate aims. Funding for the Council's activities comes from corporate British Council sources together with other partnership funding.

Funds: Contributes to Northern Irish companies touring abroad (including Republic of Ireland). Will also assist with foreign practitioners visiting Northern Ireland.

Application Procedure: No formal procedure. Applications outlining project details are accepted all year round.

CALOUSTE GULBENKIAN FOUNDATION

UK Branch, 98 Portland Place
London WIN 4ET, England
Tel: 0171 636 5313
Fax: 0171 637 3421
Contact: Siân Ede, Assistant Director, Arts

Established in Lisbon in 1956, one year after the death of Calouste Sarkis Gulbenkian, the foundation's London office deals with all applications from the United Kingdom and the Republic of Ireland.

Funds: The foundation lists the arts as one of its four current priorities and states that its arts Programme deals with the arts for adults and young people out of formal education settings. It runs two schemes for professional practitioners: 'Two Cultures - The

Arts and Science' designed to encourage professional arts groups to produce practical projects which demonstrate a creative engagement with new thinking and practice in science and technology and 'Time to Experiment' which helps professional artists or groups to devise and experiment before they perfect a project. Priority is given to projects which demonstrate a genuine ground-breaking development for the art form as a whole. The foundation also has a particular fund to assist Irish-Portuguese Cultural Relations. Applications from projects in outlying rural areas, or those which assist women, are especially welcome.

Application procedure: No standard application form is used. Applications should be made in writing to the above address at least three months before the projected starting date.

Useful Publications: *'Advice to Applicants for Grants for the UK and Ireland'.* Available from the above address.

COMMUNITY RELATIONS COUNCIL

6 Murray Street, Belfast BT1 6DN
Tel: 01232 439953
Fax: 01232 235208
E-mail: info@community-relations.org.uk
Website: http://www.community-relations.org.uk/community-relations
Contact: Ray Mullan, Information Officer

The Community Relations Council's main aim is to assist others in addressing communal divisions in Northern Ireland.

Funds: The Council administers grant schemes in the areas of media, publications, inter-community and local cultural traditions.

Application procedure: Application forms, criteria and further information are available from the above address.

Useful publications: *'A Cultural Diversity Directory'*, available from the above address.

CO-OPERATION IRELAND (formerly CO-OPERATION NORTH)

37 Upper Fitzwilliam Street, Dublin 2.
Tel: 01 6610588
Fax: 01 6618456
E-mail: info@co-operation-north.ie
Website: http://www.co-operation-north.ie
Contact: Marianne McGill, Youth, Education and Community Programme

7 Botanic Avenue, Belfast BT7 1JG
Tel: 01232 321462
Fax: 01232 247522
E-mail: info@co-operation.nireland.ie
Contact:
Malcolm Ross, EU Programme Manager

Co-operation Ireland's mission statement is 'to advance mutual understanding and respect by promoting practical co-operation between the people of Northern Ireland and the Republic of Ireland'.

Funds: Youth, Education and Community based activities on a North/South basis. Co-operation North, in association with the IBEC/CBI joint business council, also implement the EU's Special Support Programme for Peace & Reconciliation Measure 3.1 which, amongst other things, helps to develop cross-border cultural interactions within Northern Ireland and the six border counties.

Application procedure: Application forms available on request.

CULTURAL RELATIONS COMMITTEE OF IRELAND/COMHAR CULTÚRA ÉIREANN

Department of Foreign Affairs
79 St. Stephen's Green, Dublin 2
Tel: 01 4082322/4082326/4082381
Fax: 01 4082611
Contact: Maura O'Connor, Higher Executive Officer

The Cultural Relations Committee (CRC) is a voluntary, non-statutory body, established in 1949 which advises on the distribution of financial grants from the allocation for cultural relations abroad made to the Department of Foreign Affairs. Its members, who are appointed for a two-year period by the Minister, draw on a wide range of expertise and experience in cultural matters. The CRC's fund making allocation is jointly sourced from the National Lottery and Exchequer funds.

Funds: The CRC allocates grants in support of Irish cultural activity of excellence in other countries. In deciding on which events to assist the Committee considers their potential to promote tourism and investment from abroad. Particular attention is given to events staged in countries where awareness of Irish cultural and artistic achievement may not have kept pace with political or economic ties.

Application procedure: Application forms, including details of eligibility and criteria for grant aid, are available on request from the above address.

EUROPEAN COMMISSION

Irish Office, 18 Dawson Street, Dublin 2
Tel: 01 6625113
Fax: 01 6625118
Contact: Information Department

Northern Ireland Office
9-15 Bedford Street, Belfast BT2 7EG
Tel: 01232 240708
Fax: 01232 248241
Contact: Information Department

Culture 2000 Programme: The Committee to the European Parliament, the Council and the Committee of the regions have recently outlined the EU's new 'CULTURE 2000 PROGRAMME' which will guide the EU's support of the arts and cultural heritage until 2004. The programme is described as 'a single financing instrument for cultural co-operation' and is designed to replace the somewhat cumbersome KALEIDOSCOPE, ARIANE and RAPHAEL programmes with a guiding, comprehensive and simplified approach to cultural support.

Funds: The proposed new programme lists the following areas as its priorities for funding: Integrated projects covered by structured, multiannual cultural co-operation agreements; major projects with a European and/or international dimension; specific, innovative and/or experimental projects within the community and/or in non-member countries.

Application procedure: As the new programme still awaits approval by the European Parliament and Council, precise details have not been finalised and application procedures are not yet established. There is the possibility, however, of a call for selected applications later in 1998 to test the new programme.

Useful publications: *'First European Community Framework Programme in Support of Culture (2000-2004)'*. Available from Catherine Boothman (International Desk, Arts Council. Tel: 01 6180200.) *'VIA'*, the bimonthly international arts newsletter,

produced by The Arts Council, The Arts Council of Northern Ireland and The British Council, carries news and information about European Community support for culture and European Union policy which affects culture.

EC Cultural Contact Points: Catherine Boothman at the International Desk at The Arts Council/An Comhairle Ealaíon has recently been appointed as the Cultural Contact Point for Ireland. Cultural Contact Points can offer technical assistance for organisations applying to the EC for funding as well as further information about EC cultural support and policy. The British Cultural Contact Point is Tim Grange at the International Arts Bureau, London. (Tel: 0171 4036454).

FÁS TRAINING AND EMPLOYMENT AUTHORITY

Head Office, 27/33 Upper Baggot Street
Dublin 4
Tel: 01 6070500
Fax: 01 6070611
Contact:
Local FÁS Employment Services Officer

Through its Community Employment Programme, FÁS, the national body with responsibility for training and retraining, was recently reported to be indirectly funding drama and dance activities in Ireland to the extent of four and a half million pounds per annum. This funding is chanelled, primarily, through the Community Employment Programme initiative. Community Employment Programmes provide public bodies or voluntary organisations with resources to employ eligible candidates who have been unemployed for one year or more, for activities which are for community or public benefit and which provide valuable training and employment for participants.

Community Employment quotas have been reached in many parts of the country and waiting lists for schemes may be in operation.

Funds: FÁS pays a wages grant for all approved participants for the full period of employment. A contribution towards full-time supervision and material costs is made and grants towards participant development are provided. FÁS is also phasing in support to sponsor groups for the development and training skills required to manage the project and its resources.

Application procedure: Organisations are encouraged to submit a detailed plan setting out the objectives and work programme of the project. FÁS provides assistance in completing this plan.

Useful Publications: *'Sponsor Application Pack'.* Available from your local FÁS office.

INTERNATIONAL FUND FOR IRELAND

PO Box 2000, Dublin 2
Tel: 01 4780655
Fax: 01 6712116
Contact: Mr. T Russell, Joint Director General.

PO Box 2000, Belfast BT4 3SA
Tel: 01232 768832
Fax: 01232 763313
Contact: Mr. T. Codd, Joint Director General.

The International Fund for Ireland was established by the British and Irish Governments with the twin aims of promoting economic and social advance in both parts of Ireland and encouraging contact, dialogue and reconciliation throughout Ireland.

Funds: Through its various initiatives the fund supports projects which stimulate private investment and enterprise,

supplement public programmes or enhance voluntary effort including self-help schemes.

Application procedure: Application form available on request.

THE IRELAND FUNDS

Oscar Wilde House, No. 1 Merrion Square Dublin 2
Tel: 01 6627878
Fax: 01 6627879
E-Mail: ifdublin@iol.ie
Contact: Kieran McLoughlin, Director Ireland

Founded in 1976 by key American businessmen, led by Dr A J F O'Reilly, The Ireland Funds now operate in nine countries and have distributed over £50 million to numerous projects across Ireland. Supporting initiatives which advance the causes of peace, culture and charity both North and South, the funds have identified 'The enhancement of Ireland's unparalleled cultural heritage and artistic life' as one its key elements. For the coming year the Funds wish to direct their support towards seeking out excellence and innovation in arts activities within communities across the island and also in promoting a positive view of Irish culture abroad.

Funds: The fund identifies a number of areas of arts activity as priorities for funding. These include projects with a strong community element; projects which engage with the formal education system, particularly in the area of the arts and young people; artistic events or organisations which enhance the economic potential of the local economy; individual artists, including theatre and dance practitioners, who may need support at the developmental stage of their careers.

Application Procedure: The Funds entertain applications from projects, likely to meet their detailed criteria, in the first quarter of each year. Applications are accepted on an official application form only, which is available from the Funds office

Useful publications: *'The Ireland Funds: Grants Policy and Guidelines on Arts and Culture'*. Available from the above address.

LOCAL AUTHORITIES & DISTRICT COUNCILS
Most local authorities, both North and South, now employ Arts Officers who administer individual budgets of varying size and significance. Application procedures for these funds vary from authority to authority. A comprehensive list of all Local Authority Arts Officers is included in a separate section.

TRUSTS AND FOUNDATIONS
Various private trusts and foundations, including many based in Britain, fund artistic activities in Ireland. Examples of these trusts include THE ESME MITCHELL TRUST, THE CARNEGIE UNITED KINGDOM TRUST, THE NORTHERN IRELAND VOLUNTARY TRUST and THE FOUNDATION FOR SPORTS AND THE ARTS.

Useful publications: Many of these bodies are included in *'The Arts Funding Guide'* (Published by: The Directory of Social Change. Tel: 0171 2095151) and in *'The Hollis Arts Funding Handbook'* (Published by: Hollis Publishing. Tel: 0181 9771133). *'Funding for Voluntary Action'* (published by The Northern Ireland Voluntary Trust. Tel: 01232 245927) contains information on trusts particularly relevant to Northern Ireland.

funding available to individuals

funding

ARTS COUNCIL/AN CHOMHAIRLE EALAÍON AWARDS, SCHEMES AND BURSARIES

Arts Council/An Chomhairle Ealaíon administers numerous awards, scholarships and schemes available to individual theatre and dance practitioners. The following list simply indicates the different awards available. Comprehensive details are contained in *Awards & Opportunities* which is available on request from the Arts Council.

Travel Awards: Facilitate travel for the professional development of playwrights, play directors, set designers, critics and choreographers. Maximum value: £1,500.

ARTFLIGHT: Offers opportunities for people working in the arts to travel outside Ireland. Run in association with the Arts Council of Northern Ireland with the support of Aer Lingus.

'Go-See' Awards: Created in association with the British Council in Ireland, this award enables individuals to travel in Britain or Ireland, for various artistic purposes.

Arts Management Training Awards: Enable arts managers to undertake professional development in management either in Ireland or abroad. Range from £1,000 to £3,000.

Awards to Choreographers: Offered to assist Irish-based choreographers in the pursuit of their art. Range from £500 to £2,000.

Awards to Professional Dancers: Offered to Irish-based dance performance artists to take courses or study visits to advance their careers. Range from £300 to £1,000.

Awards to Professional Dance Teachers: Available to full-time professional dance teachers in Ireland to undertake further training. Range from £500 to £1,500.

Awards to Undergraduate Dance Students: Available for full-time dance training in a recognised institution. Range from £1,000 to £4,000.

Awards to Playwrights: Playwrights are eligible to apply for Bursaries in Literature which enable writers to concentrate on specific writing projects in Irish or English. Range from £3,000 to £8,000 for one-year bursaries and from £6,000 to £16,000 for two-year bursaries.

Awards to Play Directors: Available to undertake appropriate courses or to accept suitable placements with theatre managements in Ireland or overseas. Range from £1,000 to £2,000.

Awards to Designers for the Stage: Available to enable set, costume and other designers for the stage to undertake appropriate courses or to accept suitable placements with theatre managements in Ireland or overseas. Range from £500 to £5,000.

Awards for training in Acting: Available to individuals wishing to pursue a career in acting. Range from £1,000 to £3,500.

Residency Schemes: The Arts Council also operates a number of residency schemes which encourage direct contact between professional artists and different community groups, as well as advancing the career of younger artists. These schemes include the Artist in the Community scheme, the One Year Community Artist in Residence scheme, the Dance Artist in Residence scheme, the Play Directors in Residence scheme and the Writers in Residence scheme.

ARTS COUNCIL OF NORTHERN IRELAND AWARDS AND BURSARIES:

The Arts Council of Northern Ireland supports the work of individual artists through two different schemes which are listed below. Comprehensive details of both schemes are contained in 'Arts Council of Northern Ireland - Information 1999' which is available on request.

General Arts Awards in Performing and Creative Arts: These awards are available to all artists, including drama and dance practitioners, and those engaged in the direction and presentation of artistic events. Awards are made on the basis of the perceived artistic value to the individual applicant and the potential artistic development and welfare of the whole community. An upper limit of £5,000 exists for all awards.

Artist in the Community Scheme: The purpose of this scheme is to encourage the development of artistic projects involving professional artists and different community groupings. Funded projects take the form of residencies by artists as individuals, companies or cross-form groupings. Artists must have professional status and appropriate training. Applications should be made by the host organisation rather than the artist. Range from £500 to £2,000.

IRISH TIMES/ESB THEATRE BURSARY

c/o The Irish Times, 11 D'Olier Street, Dublin 2
Award: £5,000.
Open to: Irish stage actors, theatre directors and theatre designers under 25 years.
Application details: A full CV and project submission to the above address.
Closing date in 1998: 28th May.

LOCAL AUTHORITY AWARDS

Many local authorities, North and South, operate bursaries and awards for individual artists which are open to artists born, or residing in, the local authority's geographic area. Details of these schemes vary and are available from individual Arts Officers (listed separately).

SUNDAY INDEPENDENT/FORD ARTS BURSARY

Award: £5,000 in 1997
Open to: Young Irish artists, including theatre and dance practitioners.
Application details: The bursary is awarded on a non-submission basis. The recipient is selected by a panel of adjudicators, including Sunday Independent critics.

TYRONE GUTHRIE CENTRE REGIONAL BURSARY SCHEME

Award: A two-week stay at the Tyrone Guthrie Centre at Annaghmakerrig.
Open to: Artists born or resident in twenty six different local authorities, North and South.
Application details: The bursaries are administered by individual Arts Officers in association with Annaghmakerrig. Application details and deadlines vary and are available from local Arts Officers (listed separately).

IRISH
THEATRE
AWARDS

*An Act
of
Recognition*

NON-SUBMISSION AWARDS

BELFAST ARTS AWARDS

Open to: These awards were established by Belfast City Council, to reward significant artistic achievements by local individuals and organisations.

Categories: Drama, Film/TV/Video, Literature, Music, Visual Arts and Arts Partnership.

Selection Procedure: A short-list of nominations, based on events and activities within the preceding twelve months, is drawn up by a panel of judges and announced in February of each year.

Presentation/Announcement of Awards: The awards are presented at an annual Gala Dinner and Awards Ceremony.

DUBLIN FRINGE FESTIVAL AWARDS

Open to: All official entrants in the festival.

Categories: Best Production and Sexiest Show.

Selection Procedure: The winners are adjudicated by a panel of ten independent theatre practitioners.

Presentation/Announcement of Awards: The awards are announced on the last night of the festival.

EVENING HERALD /DUBLIN THEATRE FESTIVAL AWARDS

Open to: All productions participating in the Dublin Theatre Festival.

Categories: Best International Production, Best Irish Production, Best Children's Production, Best Irish Actor, Best Irish Actress.

Selection procedure: Three different adjudication panels, comprising of theatre personalities and Evening Herald readers, judge the awards.

Presentation/Announcement of Awards: The awards are announced at a special luncheon during the festival.

THE IRISH TIMES/ESB IRISH THEATRE AWARDS

Open to: Plays performed by professional theatre companies in the Republic of Ireland and Northern Ireland in each calendar year.

Categories: Best Actor, Best Actress, Best Actor in a Supporting Role, Best Actress in a Supporting Role, Best Director, Best Designer: Set, Best Designer: Costumes, Best Designer: Lighting, Best Production, Best New Play, Best Theatre Company, 'Special Tribute' Award.

Selection Procedure: Judges will attend plays which, in the first instance, have been nominated by any one of the Irish Times theatre critics. A short-list of four nominations per category will then be established.

Presentation/Announcement of Awards: The awards are presented at a gala prize-giving ceremony in Dublin.

SUNDAY INDEPENDENT/FORD ARTS AWARDS

Open to: Professional arts practitioners who are judged to be leading exponents of their art form.

Categories: Thirteen individuals were nominated in 1997, representing all the art forms.

Selection procedure: Individuals are selected by a committee made up of The Sunday Independent's various critics and chaired by the paper's Arts Editor, Mr. Ronan Farren.

Presentation/Announcement of Awards: A number of nominees are featured in individual interviews which are carried by the paper over the period of the competition. The awards are then formally presented at a ceremony in Dublin, which usually takes place in November of each year.

SUNDAY TRIBUNE ARTS AWARDS

Open to: All professional theatre productions presented in Ireland, North and South, in each calendar year.

Categories: Categories vary from year to year but usually include: Best Production, Best Performances and Best New Play.

Selection procedure: The Awards are decided by The Sunday Tribune's theatre and arts critics.

Presentation/Announcement of Awards: The awards are listed in the Sunday Tribune at the end of each year. There is no official awards ceremony.

SUBMISSION AWARDS:

A.I.B. BETTER IRELAND AWARDS

c/o AIB Nationwide Better Ireland Awards
Bankcentre, Ballsbridge, Dublin 4

Awards: 25 local awards of £1,000 each, 6 recognition awards of £4,000 each, 1 overall category award of £20,000, 1 overall winning group award of £50,000.

Open to: Projects that encourage standards of excellence in various areas of the arts, including theatre and dance.

Application procedure: Application forms available from the above address or from any AIB branch.

Closing date in 1998: 22nd May.

BASS IRELAND ARTS AWARD

c/o Awards Secretary, Arts Council of Northern Ireland
MacNeice House, 77 Malone Road
Belfast BT9 6AQ

Award: £5,000

Open to: Individuals or groups in all branches of the arts in Northern Ireland.

Application procedure: Application forms available from the above address.

Closing date in 1998: 28th August.

COTHÚ ARTS SPONSOR OF THE YEAR AWARDS

c/o Cothú - The Business Council for the Arts
64 Lower Mount Street, Dublin 2

Awards: £2,500 Ernst & Young Arts Award to the arts organisation making the most effective and imaginative use of arts sponsorship. Awards made to sponsors include: Best Arts Sponsorship by a Small Business; Best Continuing Sponsorship of the Arts; Best Sponsorship of a Single Arts Project, Best Arts Sponsorship in the Community.

Open to: All businesses, large and small, engaging in imaginative and effective sponsorship of the arts.

Application procedure: Nomination form available from the above address.

Closing date in 1998: 7th September.

PLAYWRIGHTING AWARDS:

THE IRELAND FUNDS ANNUAL LITERARY AWARD

c/o The Ireland Funds, Oscar Wilde House
No. 1 Merrion Square, Dublin 2

Competition details: An annual, non-submission award for outstanding work. Presented by the American Ireland Fund.

Prize: £10,000.

OIREACHTAS LITERARY AWARDS

c/o Stiúrthóir an Oireachtais
6 Sráid Fhearchair, Baile Átha Cliath 2

Competition details: Playwrighting awards include: Full-Length Play Award (sponsored by The National Theatre Society Ltd.); One Act Play Award (sponsored by Amharclann de hÍde); Údarás na Gaeltachta One Act Play Award.

Prizes: £1,000, £500 and £500 respectively.

Entry fee: £10 per play.

Closing date in 1998: 1st July.

O.Z. WHITEHEAD PLAY COMPETITION

c/o Society of Irish Playwrights
Irish Writers' Centre, Dublin 1

Competition details: One-act play competition open to Irish playwrights and foreigners resident in Ireland.

Prizes: £500 (1st), £250 (2nd), £100 (3rd).

Entry fee: £10 per play.

Closing date: Spring/Summer.

P.J. O'CONNOR RADIO DRAMA AWARDS

c/o Radio Centre, R.T.E. Dublin 4

Competition details: Thirty minute radio drama competition.

Prizes: £1,000 and broadcast (1st), broadcast (runners-up), £250 (Six additional plays selected for Amateur Drama Radio Festival)

Entry fee: None.

Closing date: Oct/Nov.

STEWART PARKER TRUST PLAYWRIGHTING BURSARIES

Stewart Parker Trust
Institute of Irish Studies
Queens University, University Road
Belfast BT7 1NN

Competition details: The trust identifies new writers in receipt of their first professional production in each calendar year. Nominations are accepted from professional theatre companies only.

Prizes: Stewart Parker New Playwright Bursary (£7,500); BBC Radio Drama Award (£1,000 plus an invitation to submit a play for production); BBC Radio Drama Award in the Irish Language (£1,000 plus an invitation to submit a play for production). Community Relations Award - for a play contributing to community relations in Ireland (£3,000). Plays qualifying for The Community Relations award must have been presented in Northern Ireland.

VERY SPECIAL ARTS YOUNG PLAYWRIGHT PROGRAMME

c/o City Arts Centre, 23-25 Moss Street, Dublin 2

Competition details: Plays on the theme of disability, with a maximum of four actors are accepted from groups or individuals aged 15-18 or from those still in full-time secondary education.

Prize: A full production, co-produced by Very Special Arts and the National Theatre Society, and a tour of the play, both North and South.

Entry fee: £35 for participation in the entire programme which includes a number of day-long workshops facilitated by practising playwrights and theatre directors.

Closing date in 1998: 27th November.

The Ballet Theatre Ireland College of Dance
Bellevue , Glenbrook, Co Cork
Tel/Fax: 021 842043
Course: 2/3 year full time professional dance diploma

Belfast Institute of Further and Higher Education (BIFHE)
College Square East, Belfast BT1 6DJ
Tel: 01232 265265
Fax: 01232 265451
Courses: Wide variety of courses at differing academic levels

Betty Ann Norton Theatre School
Clonbrock House
11 Harcourt Street, Dublin 2
Tel: 01 4751913 / 4758813
Fax: 01 4751140
Courses: Two year acting diploma course

Bray V.E.C.
Town Hall, Unit 1, Market Court
Bray, Co. Wicklow
Tel: 01 2862482
Course: 2 year post leaving certificate diploma course in Performing Arts

Central Technical Institute
Parnell Street, Waterford
Tel: 051 874007
Course: 1 year post leaving certificate in Drama Studies

Coláiste Dhulaigh
Clonshaugh Road, Dublin 17
Tel: 01 8474399
Courses: 2 year post leaving certificate in Drama Studies (NCVA)

Coláiste Stiofán Noafa
Tramore Road, Cork
Tel: 021 961020

Course: 1 year post leaving certificate in Drama Studies
2 year diploma post leaving certificate in Professional Dance

College of Commerce
Sydenham Rd., Dundrum, Dublin 14
Tel: 01 2982340
Courses: 1 year post leaving certificate in Drama Studies (NCVA)

College of Dance
Devalois House, 5 Meeting Hse Lane
Marys Abbey, Dublin 7
Tel: 01 8735536
Courses: 2 year full time diploma in professional dance

The Dance Studio
72 Beatrice Road, Bangor BT20 5DL
Tel: 01247 457163
Course: 3 year dancer/teacher training course - Diploma from the Royal Academy of Dancing

Gaiety School of Acting
Meeting House Square
Temple Bar, Dublin 2
Tel: 01 6799277
Course: 2 year full time acting course.

Inchicore Vocational School
Emmet Road, Dublin 8
Tel: 01 4535358
Course: 2 year post leaving certificate in Drama Studies

Liberties College (Bull Alley) V.E.C.
Bull Alley Street, Dublin 8
Tel: 01 4540044
Course: 2 year post leaving certificate in Drama Studies (NCVA)

Marino V.E.C.
Marino Mart, Dublin 3
Tel: 01 8332100
Courses: 1 year post leaving certificate in Drama Studies

Regional Technical College
Dublin Road, Dundalk, Co. Louth
Tel: 042 70200
Course: 3 year diploma in cultural studies

Samuel Beckett Centre
Trinity College, Dublin 1
Tel: 01 7022266
Courses: 3 year degree in Drama and Theatre Studies. 4 year degree in Theatre Studies

Senior College
Ballyfermot Road
Ballyfermot, Dublin
Tel: 01 6269421
Course: 1 year post leaving certificate course in Performing Arts

University College Dublin
Belfield, Dublin 4
Tel: 01 7067632 (Arts Admin)
/01 7068049 (Drama Studies)
Courses: Higher diploma in Arts Administration
M.A. and Higher diploma in Drama Studies

University of Ulster
Cromore Road, Coleraine
Co Londonderry BT52 1SA
Tel: 01265 44141
Course: 3 year degree in Theatre Studies

Support Organisations

Amateur Drama Council of Ireland
Griffith St., Athlone, Co. Westmeath
Tel: 0902 72333
Fax: 0902 72333
Contact: Colm Kelly

Association for Business Sponsorship of the Arts (ABSA)
PO Box 496, Danesfort
120 Malone Road, Belfast BT9 5GL
Tel: 01232 664736
Fax: 01232 664500
Contact: Hilary McGrady

Association of Drama Adjudicators
Rue de Bac, Mill Grov
Delgany, Co. Wicklow
Tel: 01 2874280/2871373
Contact: Myles Purcell

Association of Professional Dancers in Ireland
De Valois House
5 Meeting House Lane
off Mary's Abbey, Dublin 7
Tel: 01 8730288
Fax: 01 8730288
email prodance@iol.ie
Contact: Karen Hennessy

CAFE (Creative Activity for Everyone)
143 Townsend Street, Dublin 2
Tel: 01 6770330
Fax: 01 6713268
Contact: Simeon Smith

Cothú - The Business Council for the Arts
64 Lower Mount Street, Dublin 2
Tel: 01 6766966
Fax: 01 6766997
Contact: Gerard AE Watson

Cultural Business Network
Artservices, 17a Ormeau Avenue
Belfast BT2 8HD
Tel: 01232 237717
Fax: 01232 237717
Email: cbn@artservicesireland.com
Contact: Mark Robinson/Anne Kennedy

Dance Collective
34 Station Road
Sydenham, Belfast BT4 1RF
Tel: 01232 653541
Fax: 01232 286025
Contact: Anthea McWilliams

Department of Arts, Heritage, Gaeltacht and the Islands
Dún Aimhirgin, Mespil Road
Dublin 4, Ireland
Tel: 01 6670788
Fax: 01 6670825
Contact: Cian Ó Lionáin

The Drama League of Ireland
P.O. Box 3094, Dublin 8
Tel: 01 4530369/4734814
Fax: 01 4530369
E-Mail: mpearsiatairl@tinet.ie
Contact: Mary Pears

Firkin Crane Dance Development Centre
Shandon, Cork
Tel: 021 507487
Fax: 021 501124
Contact: Mary Brady

Irish Actors Equity Group
SIPTU, Liberty Hall, Dublin 1
Tel: 01 8740081
Fax: 01 8743691
Contact: Gerald Brown

Irish Literature Exchange
Irish Writers Centre
19 Parnell Square, Dublin 1
Tel: 01 8727900
Fax: 01 8727875
Contact: Marc Cabal

Irish Theatre Archive Ltd.
c/o Civic Museum
58 South William Street, Dublin 2
Tel: 01 6775877
Tel: 01 6775954

Irish Writers Centre
19 Parnell Square, Dublin 1
Tel: 01 8721302
Fax: 01 8726282
Contact: Jacinta Douglas

National Association of Youth Drama
34 Upper Gardiner Street, Dublin 1.
Tel: 01 8781301
Fax: 01 8781302
Contact: Eilis Mullen

Northern Amateur Theatre Association
49 Beverly Gardens, Bangor
Co. Down BT20 4NQ
Tel: 01247 455819
Contact: Tony Coghlan

Society of Irish Playwrights
Irish Writers Centre
19 Parnell Square, Dublin 1
Tel: 01 8721302
Fax: 01 8726282
Contact: Ted Gannon

The Theatre Shop
5-6 Sth Great Georges St., Dublin 2
Tel: 01 6719278
Fax: 01 6719301
Email: roughmag@iol.ie
Website: www.theatreshop.ie
Contact: Martin Munroe

suppliers & services

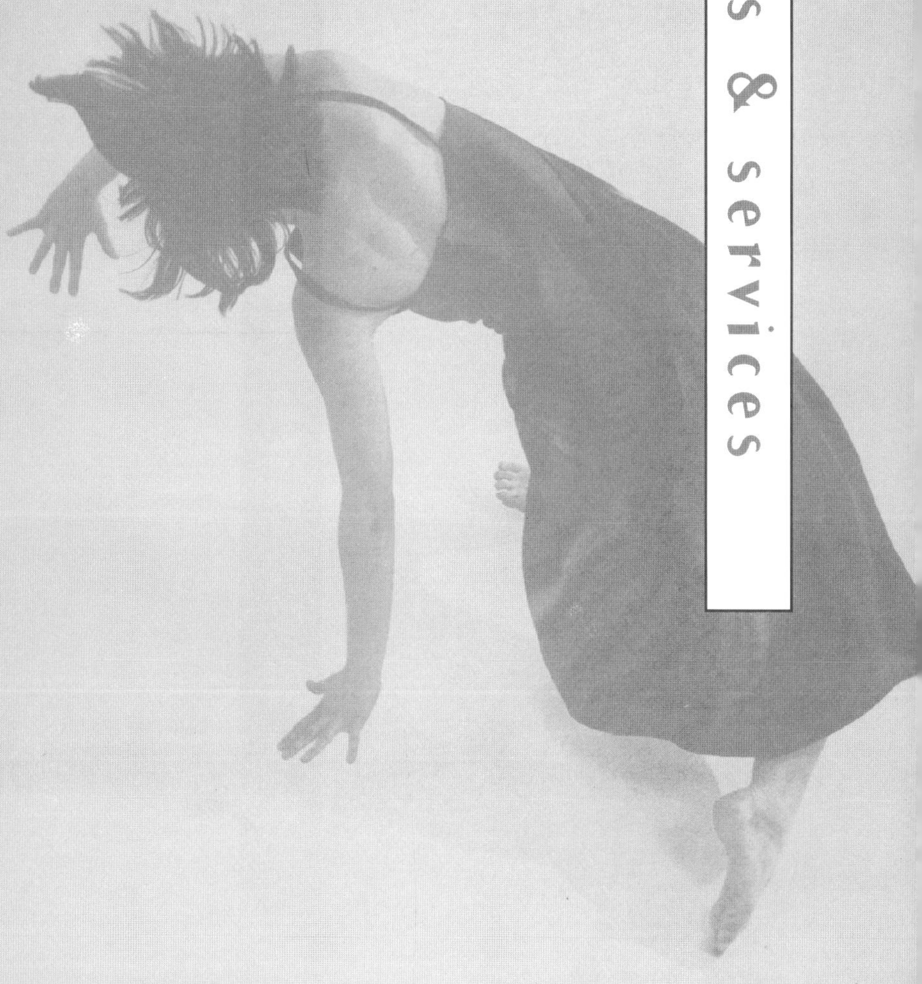

Agents And Management Services

The AGENCY
47 Adelaide Road, Dublin 2.
Tel: 01 661 8535
Fax: 01 676 0052
Contact: Teri Hayden

Allsorts Agency
Pelletstown House, Ashtown Gate,
Ashtown, Dublin 15.
Tel: 01 8682329
Fax: 01 838630
Contact: Anne Marie McCormack

The Ann Curtis Agency
101 Collins Avenue East, Dublin 9
Tel: 01 8551112
Fax: 01 8551146
Contact: Ann Curtis

Ashdown Associates
Crescent Arts Centre
2-4 University Rd., Belfast BT7 1NH.
Tel: 01232 248861
Contact: Donal McKendry

Betty Ann Norton
Clonbrock House
11 Harcourt Street, Dublin 2
Tel: 01 4751913 / 4758813
Fax: 01 4751150
Contact: Betty Ann Norton

Castaway Actors Agency
30/31 Wicklow Street, Dublin 2
Tel: 01 6719264
Fax: 01 6719133
Centre Stage Agency
7 Rutledge Terrace
South Circular Road, Dublin 8
Tel: 01 4533599
Contact: Geraldine Dunne

First Call Management
29/30 Dame Street, Dublin 2
Tel: 01 6798401
Fax: 01 6798353
Contact: Maureen McGlynn

Fixers
121 Grange Road
Rathfarnham, Dublin 14
Tel & Fax: 01 4933076
Mobile: 088 2602427
Contact: Yvette Hally

Hanna Greenfield
3 Wellington Park Avenue
Belfast BT9 6DT, Northern Ireland
Tel: 0232 664030
Fax: 0232 665644
Contact: Hilary Hanna

LBM
Lorraine Brennan Management
*currently moving office
Tel: 01 4562826
Fax: 01 4650339
Contact: Lorraine Brennan

The Lisa Richards Agency
The Basement,
15 Lower Pembroke Street, Dublin 2
Tel: 01 6624880
Fax: 01 6624884

Personal Management Services
5 Ballmiscaw Cottage, Holywood
Co. Down BT18 9RT
Tel: 0232 761423
Contact: Peter McVea

Re: Actors Co-Operative Agency
1 Eden Quay, Dublin 1
Tel: 01 8786833
Fax: 01 8783182
E-mail: reactors@tinet.ie
Contact: Una Kavanagh

Theresa Nolan Agency
14 Beech Grove, Booterstown Ave.
Blackrock, Co. Dublin
Tel: 01 2881537
Fax: 01 2881541
E-Mail: teresanolan@tinet.ie
Mobile: 088 514385
Contact: Theresa Nolan

Maeve Widger
19 Whitebarn Road
Churchtown, Dublin 14
Tel: 01 2986636
Contact: Maeve Widger

Arts Consultants

Artbeat Management Services
16 Old Devon Park
Lower Salthill, Galway
Contact: Jane Daly
Tel/Fax: 091 527026
Mobile: 087 2463399

Arts Services Northern Ireland
17A Ormeau Ave., Belfast BT2 8HD
Contact: Mark Robinson
Tel/Fax: 01232 237717
e-mail:
info@artservicesireland.com
Website:
http://artservicesireland.com

Jan Branch
27 Pretoria Street
Belfast BT9 5AQ
Tel: 01232 666995

Annette Clancy
2 York Avenue, Rathgar, Dublin 6
Mobile: 087 2635363
E-mail: annettec@iol.ie

Anne Kelly
Arts Administration Studies
University College Dublin
Belfield, Dublin 4
Tel: 01 7067632

Emer McNamara
188 Clontarf Rd., Clontarf, Dublin 3
Tel / Fax: 01 833 1078
Mobile: 087 2419536
E-mail: emermc@tinet.ie

Maura O' Keefe
14 Summerville Park
Upper Rathmines Road, Dublin 6
Tel: 087 2234201

Maurice Power
Theatre and Production Consultant
1 Kevins Avenue
Strandhill Road, Sligo
Tel / Fax: 071 69371
Mobile: 087 2607327

Costume Designers

Joan Bergin
The Costume Mill
1 Rowsertown Lane
Kilmainham, Dublin 8
Tel: 01 6795485
Mobile: 086 2575091

Joan Cleary
11 Belmount Avenue
Donnybrook, Dublin 4
Tel: 01 2696075
Mobile: 087 2269214

Johanna Connor
c/o Bedrock Theatre Company
36-37 Lower Ormond Quay, Dublin 1
Tel: 01 8729300
Fax: 01 8729478
E-mail: bedrock@clubi.ie

Dennis Darcy Costume Tailor
65 Capel Street, Dublin 1
Tel: 01 8732256

Moggie Douglas
Possextown, Enfield, Co Meath
Tel: 0405 41655
Mobile: 087 2355783

Monica Ennis
Clooncagh
New Inn, Ballinasloe, Co Galway
Tel: 0905 77938
Mobile: 087 2428937

Sheila Fahey Costumer Supervisor
2 Hadleigh Court, Haddington Road
Ballsbridge, Dublin 4
Tel: 01 6686072
Mobile: 086 602907

Jacqueline Kobler
Garden Flat
40 Upper Leeson Street, Dublin 2
Tel: 01 660 6904
Mobile: 088 2165653

Des Leach Costumier/Tailor
3 Cavendish Row, Dublin 1
Tel: 01 8746330

Sadie Looney
24 Riverside Avenue
Clonshaugh, Dublin 17
Mobile: 087 2273147

Leonore McDonagh
6 Church Avenue South
South Circular Road, Dublin 8
Mobile: 087 2731162

Grainne O'Connor
28 Belgrave Road
Monkstown, Co Dublin
Tel: 061 8328477
Mobile: 086 2419538

Anne O'Halloran
Costume Cutter / Supervisor
57 Orwell Gardens, Dublin 14
Tel: 01 4924973

Katherine Sankey
26 Bloomfield Avenue
Portabello
Dublin 8
Tel: 01 4535639

Kathy Strachan
21 Sorrento Court,
Dalkey, Co Dublin
Tel: 01 2849674
Mobile: 087 2692277

Joe Vanek
15 Arnott Street
Dublin 8
Tel: 01 4731186
Fax: 01 4731186

Graphic Designers

A&D Design, Advertising and
Consultancy
Envision House
Flood Street, Galway
Tel: 091 561370
Fax: 091 561379
E-mail: addesign@iol.ie
Contact: Larry Hynes / Idé
Deloughry

ArtServices
McAvoy House, 17A Ormeau Avenue
Belfast BT2 8HD
Tel: 01232 237717
Fax: 01232 237717
E-mail:
infor@artservicesireland.com
Website:
http://artservicesireland.com

Bite Associates
Fitzgerald House
Grand Parade, Cork
Tel: 021 275988
Fax: 021 278508
E-mail: biteass@tinet.ie
Contact: Lisa Sheridan

Image Now
Image Now House
Little Fitzwilliam Place
off Fitzwilliam Lane, Dublin 2
Tel: 01 6795251
Fax: 01 6627985
E-mail: post@imagenow.ie
Contact: Anne Brady

Public Communications Centre
22 South Great Georges Street
Dublin 2
Tel: 01 6794173
Fax: 01 6795409
E-mail: pcc@iol.ie
Contact: Ann Sheridan

Lighting Designers

ACK Productions
22 Alexandra Park,
Holywood Co. Down BT18 9ET
Tel: 01232 421513
Fax: 01232 423084
Mobile: 0802 642029
e-mail: kerrac@ackprod.dnet.co.uk
Contact: Alister Kerr

Debbie Behan
32 Primrose Avenue
Phibsboro, Dublin 7
Tel: 01 860 0359
Mobile: 087 2362413

Aideen Cosgrove
25 Landsdown Park, Dublin 4
Mobile: 087 2384576

Lee Davis
21 Reuben Street
Dolphins Barn, Dublin 8
Tel: 01 4547899
Pager: 1550 183049

Wayne Farrell
84c Southwell Road
Bangor

Co Down BT20 3AE
Tel: 01247 454052
Email: nelper@hotmail.com

Mark Gallione
32 Primrose Avenue, Dublin 7
Mobile: 086 2611512

Paul Keogan
5 St James Terrace
Sandymount Road
Dublin 4
Tel/Fax: 01 6681153
Mobile: 087 2434352
E-mail: keogs@indigo.ie

Tina MacHugh
27 Beauvale, Ferdinand Street
London NW1 8EY, England
Tel: 0171 4821233
Agent: Clare Vidal-Hall.
Tel: 0181 7417647

Nick McCall
4 Ann Devlin Park
Rathfarnham, Dublin 14
Mobile: 087 2298181

Stephen McManus
3 Salisbury Gardens
Belfast BT15 5EL
Mobile: 087 2442 009

Paul O'Neill
Studio 9
The Firestation Artists Studio
9 - 11 Lower Buckingham Street
Dublin 1.
Tel: 01 8550128
Fax: 01 8555176

John Riddell
24 Red Car Street
Belfast BT6 9BP
Tel: 01232 222439
Mobile: 0410 538612

Conleth White
174c Orwell Road, Dublin 14
Tel: 01 4547899
Pager: 1550 183049

Paul Winters
3, Dalymount
Phibsborough, Dublin 7
Tel: 01 6713387
Mobile: 087 2682983

Photographers

Arthur Gough
2 Broad Street, Limerick
Tel: 061 313139/310874
Mobile: 086 8381366

Chris Hill Photographic
17 Clarence Street, Belfast BT2 8DY
Tel: 01232 245038
Fax: 01232 231942
E-mail: ChrisHillPhotograpic@
btinternet.com

Aengus McMahon
6 Father Griffin Avenue, Galway
Tel/Fax: 091 589148

Ronnie Norton
21 Creighton Street, Dublin 2
Tel: 01 6712500
Fax: 01 6712539

Vinny O'Byrne
The Rear, Regal House
Fitzwilliam Street
Ringsend, Dublin 4.
Tel: 01 6685283

Provision
6 Cornmarket Street, Cork
Contact: Michael MacSweeney
Tel: 021 272884
Mobile: 087 2557884/087 2208855
Fax: 021 271547

Aoife Rice
Arus Brid, Thornhill, Maynooth Rd
Celbridge, Co. Kildare
Tel: 01 6273496
Mobile: 086 8103700

Derek Spiers
Tel: 01 8558154

Amelia Stein
4 Camden Market
Grantham Street, Dublin 8
Tel: 01 4751275
Fax: 01 4780396

Michael Taylor
412 Beersbridge Road
Belfast BT5 5EB
Tel: 01232 654450
Fax: 01232 471625
Mobile: 0850 663089

Poster Distribution

Blackthorn Art
13b Echlin Street, Dublin 8
Tel: 01 4536711
Contact: Stephen Holland

Trish Connolly
14 Turlock Árd, Westside, Galway
Tel: 091 528675

Diane Henshaw
32A Fitzroy Avenue, Belfast BT7 1HY
Tel: 01232 330113/243145

Irish Poster Advertising
Merchants Court
24 Merchants Quay, Dublin 8
Tel: 01 6798060
Fax: 01 6797495

Main Event Posters Ltd.
The Stockyard
20 Sheriff Street, Dublin 1
Tel: 01 8556684
Fax: 01 8552053

Muriel Todd
Info Desk, Belfast Central Library
Royal Avenue, Belfast
Tel: 01232 243233 ext 277

Production / Technical Management

Ingrid Arthurf
12c Ashley Avenue, Belfast BT9 7BT
Tel: 01232 381843/666945
Mobile: 0410 932974

John Ashton
Raford, Killtulegh
Athenry, Co Galway
Mobile: 087 2426070
Fax: 091 563905
E-mail: macnas@iol.ie

Stephen Bourke
21 Reuben Street
Dolphins Barn, Dublin 8
Mobile: 087 2489338
Fax: 01 8729478

Tony Collins
Mobile: 087 2509524

Lee Davis
21 Reuben Street
Dolphins Barn, Dublin 8
Tel: 01 4547899
Pager: 1550 183049

Mark Gallione
32 Primrose Avenue
Dublin 7
Mobile: 086 2611512

Brendan Galvin
15 Glincook Park, Maglin Road
Ballincollig, Co Cork
Tel: 021 872318
Mobile: 087 2475954
E-mail: bjgalvin@aol.com

Nick McCall
4 Ann Devlin Park
Rathfarnham, Dublin 14
Mobile: 087 2298181

Maurice Power
Production Consultant
1 Kevins Avenue
Strandhill Road, Sligo
Tel/Fax: 071 69371
Mobile: 087 2607327

Brian Reilly
67 Bryansburn Road
Bangor, Co Down BT20 3SD
Tel: 01247 275759
Mobile: 410 014450

Theatre Production Services
9 Emerald Square
Cork Street, Dublin 8
Contact: Pat Byrne / Paul Foley
Tel: 01 4546815
Mobile: 086 2604966

Conleth White
Mobile: 087 2316464

Paul Winters
3, Dalymount
Phibsborough, Dublin 7
Tel: 01 6713387
Mobile: 087 2682983

Public Relations/ Publicity

Kate Bowe PR
50 South William Street, Dublin 2.
Tel: 01 67136727
Fax: 01 6773224

Mary Folan
Publicist
7 South Great Georges Street
Dublin 2
Tel: 01 6704907
Fax: 01 6704908
Mobile: 087 2434816

Maureen Kennelly
Public Relations and Event
Management
c/o Fishamble Theatre Company
Shamrock Chambers
Eustace Street, Dublin 2
Tel: 086 8291179

Kearney O Keefe
11 Marlboro Street, Cork.
Tel: 021 278580
Mobile: 087 2527495
Fax: 021 278581
E-mail: kearney@cit.ie
Contact: Ivor Melia

Rose Parkinson PR
34 Herbert Street, Dublin 2
Tel: 01 6776565

Carmel White
Media Reach Public Relations
Consultants
34 Belgrave Square, Dublin 6
Tel: 01 4961494/4962949
Fax: 01 4968388
E-Mail: carmelwhite@tinet.ie

Set Designers
Barbara Bradshaw
15 Riversdale Grove
K.C.R., Dublin 6
Tel: 01 4929426

Johanna Connor
c/o Bedrock Theatre Company
36-37 Lower Ormond Quay
Dublin 1
Tel: 01 8729300
Fax: 01 8729478
E-mail: bedrock@clubi.ie

David Craig
3 Shore Street
Donaghadee, Co Down BT21 0DG
Tel: 01247 883826
Mobile: 0780 1650545

Moggie Douglas
Possextown, Enfield, Co Meath
Tel: 0405 41655
Mobile: 087 2355783

Monica Frawley
26 Primrose Street
The Broadstone, Dublin 7
Tel: 01 8600872
or
37 Rue de la Dysse
Montpeyroux, 34150 France
Tel: 0033 46788 966671

Frank Halloran Flood
27 Rivervalley Rise
Swords, Co Dublin
Tel: 01 8402312
Mobile: 088 2506854

Ben Hennessy
33 Morley Terrace, Waterford
Tel: 051 384325

Fiona Leech
33 Greenville Terrace, Dublin 8
Tel: 01 4532885
E-mail: jjvernon@hotmail.com

Terry Loane
3 Pirrie Park Gardens
Belfast BT6 0AG
Tel: 01232 461260

Blaithin Sheerin
4 Greenfield Place
Harolds Cross, Dublin 6
Tel: 01 4979031

Kathy Strachan
21 Sorrento Court

Dalkey, Co Dublin
Tel: 01 2849674
Mobile: 087 2692277

First Stage
Set and Event Design
56 Camden Street Lower
Dublin 2
Tel: 01 4782800
Fax: 01 4784353
E-mail: qaarch@iol.ie

Katherine Sankey
26 Bloomfield Avenue
Portabello
Dublin 8
Tel: 01 4535639

Joe Vanek
15 Arnott Street
Dublin 8
Tel: 01 4731186
Fax: 01 4731186

Sound Designers
Bell Helicopter
30 Whites Square
London SW4 7JL, England.
Tel: 0171 6278817
Contact: Conor Kelly

Dave Nolan
c/o The Abbey Theatre
26 Lower Abbey Street, Dublin 2
Tel/Fax: 01 6770254/01 8748741
E-mail: clupo@indigo.ie

Paul Keogan
5 St James Terrace
Sandymount Road, Dublin 4
Tel/Fax: 6681153
Mobile: 087 2434352
E-mail: keogs@indigo.ie

JJ Vernon
33 Greendale Terrace, Dublin 8
Tel: 01 453 2885
E-mail: jjvernon@hotmail.com

Technical Suppliers

ACK Productions
22 Alexandra Park
Holywood, Co. Down BT18 9ET
Tel: 01232 421513
Fax: 01232 423084
Mobile: 0802 642029
E-mail: kerrac@ackprod.dnet.co.uk
Contact: Alister Kerr

Aquarius Sound and Lighting
Main Street, Leixlip, Co Kildare
Tel: 01 6243382
Fax: 01 6245711
Contact: Niall Connelly

Arena Lighting
13 Castleforbes Road
North Wall, Dublin 1
Tel: 01 8554490
Fax: 01 8554868
E-mail: arena@tinet.ie
Contact: Michael Deegan

Audio International
14 Kennilworth Lane
Rathmines, Dublin 6
Tel: 01 4964066
Fax: 01 4910345
E-mail: audiointernational@tinet.ie
Contact: Pat O Brien

Black Light (Ireland) Ltd
Unit 3a, Block 8
Ballyvane Industrial Estate, Galway
Tel: 091 771679
Mobile: 087 2594277
E-mail: blacklightireland@tinet.ie
Contact: David Murphy

Continental Lasers (U.K.) Ltd
B105 Portview Trade Centre
310 Newtownards Road
Belfast BT4 1HE
Tel: 01232 458658
Fax: 01232 461550
E-mail: info@cluk.dinet.co.uk

Coverup Limited
63A Heather Road
Sandyford Industrial Estate
Sandyford, Dublin 18
Tel/Fax: 01 2952027
Contact: Bernard Dempsey

Dervan Sound
Abbey Lane, Loughrea, Co Galway
Tel: 091 841581
Fax: 091 843322
Contact: Mike Dervan

Dundrum Lighting
Main Street, Dundrum, Dublin 14
Tel: 01 2951857
Fax: 01 2951861
E-mail: lighting@iol.ie
Website:
http://ourworld.compuserve.com/h
omepages/lighting

G&R Fire Retardant Services
Unit H2, Chapelizod Industrial Est.
Dublin 20
Tel: 01 6234363
Fax: 01 6234372
Contact: Gerard Hutton

News Extracts
7 Ely Place, Dublin 2
Tel: 01 6616966
Fax: 01 6615361
E-mail: newsext@indigo.ie
Contact: Stephen Cousins

Nightshift Sound Systems Ltd
The Quay, Ballina, Co Mayo
Tel: 096 22490

Joe O'Neill Ltd
Glenamaddy, Co Galway
Tel: 0907 59022
Fax: 0907 59409
Contact: Joe Conniffe/Michael
O Hara/Martin O'Boyle/Joe O Neill

Ray Thompson Limited
8 Lorne Street, Belfast BT9 7DU
Tel: 01232 664411
Fax: 01232 664831
Contact: Phillip Marks

Session Hire
10 Upper Grand Canal Street
Dublin 4
Tel: 01 6606777
Fax: 01 6607086
Contact: Ray or Eddie

Stage Services North
Unit 10, 6-16 Duncrue Crescent
Belfast BT3 9BW
Tel: 01232 777668
Fax: 01232 771707
Contact: R Forster

Wigs & Hairdressers

Eileen Buggy
Theatrical Hair and Make Up
Mobile: 087 2688313

Patsie Giles
Theatrical Hair and Make Up
Mobile: 087 2603808

Val Sherlock
Theatrical Hair, Wig and Make up
110 Baggot Street Lower, Dublin 2
Tel: 01 6764199
Mobile: 087 2528346

Appendix 1. New Irish Plays 1988 – 1998

Appendix 2. New Irish Dance Works 1988 – 1998

Appendix 3. New Irish Operas 1988 – 1998

Please note: The following appendices list the work presented by the subsidised companies in the Irish Theatre Handbook only. The information contained was supplied by the companies themselves. Any gaps that exist are due to insufficient information being available.

Contact details: Unless otherwise stated, further information on any of the plays, dance works or operas listed is available from the relevant production company. Full contact details for all companies are included in 'Subsidised Companies'.

Appendix 1 New Irish Plays 1988 - 1998

AISLING GHÉAR

Year	Title	Author	Cast Size
1996	Republica	Aodh Ó Dhomhnaill	2

A dark and powerful drama set in a small country in South Africa, full of humour and sadness.

AMHARCLANN DE HÍDE

Year	Title	Author	Cast Size
1993	Tine Chnámh	Liam Ó Muirthile	6

An adaptation of the author's poetry with an emphasis on dance and music.

| 1993 | Mallachtúi Muintíre | Pádraic Ó Conaire | 8 |

Three of the author's short stories brought to the stage by director Michael Scott.

| 1994 | Dún na mBan trí Thine | Éilis Ní Dhuibhne | 7 |

An exploration of contemporary male/female relationships with undercurrents of myth and folklore.
Published by: Cois Life Teo Book Title: Milseog an Tsamhraidh & Dún na mban Trí Thine

| 1994 | Ceacht Houdini | Michael Harding | 4 |

Cross border politics examined in an imaginative and at times, surreal format.

| 1995 | An Solas Dearg | Antoine Ó Flatharta | 6 |

The complex world of bilingualism and the occasionally fraught relationship between the Gaeltacht and the Galltacht is explored with humour and understanding.

| 1995 | Fear an Tae | Liam Ó Muirthile | 8 |

A compassionate look at the secret world of a mental hospital as patients struggle to help themselves and each other.

| 1997 | Buille an Phíce | Brian Ó Riagáin | 5 |

An intense and at times disturbing look at the issues of power and aggression within a marriage.

| 1997 | Milseog an tSamhraidh | Éilis Ní Dhuibhne | 6 |

Two sisters flee famine Ireland and their journey from poverty becomes one of personal liberation.
Published by: Cois Life Teo Book Title: Milseog an Tsamhraidh & Dún na mban Trí Thine

THE ARK, A CULTURAL CENTRE FOR CHILDREN
(see also New Irish Operas - Appendix 3)

Year	Title	Author	Cast Size
1996	The Croons	Devised by the company	3

A music theatre show for 4-6 year olds about the last creatures to leave the Ark.

| 1997 | Out The Back Door | Barabbas.. the company | 3 |

A sixty minute piece of visual/physical theatre for older children commissioned by The Ark from Barabbas... the company.

BARABBAS... THE COMPANY

Year	Title	Author	Cast Size
1993	Come Down from the Mountain, John Clown, John Clown.	Devised by the company	3

A full-length 'red-nose' play exploring the lives of three Irish clowns.

Year	Title	Author	Cast Size
1994	Half Eight Mass of a Tuesday	Barabbas	3 +1 puppeteer

A look at the lives of a small rural congregation in the structure of a weekday mass. Uses actors and puppets.

| 1995 | Sick, Dying, Dead, Buried, Out. | Barabbas | 2 |

Follows the public and personal lives of two friends, Ultan and Padraig. Rednose. Wordless.

| 1996 | Strokehauling | Barabbas | 1 |

A very physical look at the outer and inner life of a small town draper's assistant.

| 1997 | Out the Back Door. (co-produced with The Ark) | Barabbas | 3 |

A show for families exploring children's imagination and world of play. Wordless.

BARNSTORM - KILKENNY THEATRE ARTS

Year	Title	Author	Cast Size
1996	Digger, Doc & Dee Dee.	Maeve Ingoldsby	6 + 2 musicians

A play for 6 to 12 year olds which explores many issues including bullying, and the conflicting demands on the time of a single mother and children's need for affection and attention.
Contact: Firstcall Management, 29/30 Dame Street, Dublin 2. Tel: 01 6798401.

| 1997 | Bananas In The Bread Bin. | Maeve Ingoldsby | 6 + band |

A play for 6 to 12 year olds which takes a light-hearted but insightful look at conflict and the role it plays in ordinary lives.
Contact: Firstcall Management, 29/30 Dame Street, Dublin 2. Tel: 01 6798401.

| 1997 | The 'Comer Story. | Ken Bourke | 28 |

A Community Theatre play which is a celebration of Castlecomer, its people, its history and its individual sense of identity.
Contact: Ken Bourke, Quinsboro, Monasterevin, Co. Kildare. Tel: 045-525049.

| 1998 | Silly Bits of Sky. | Maeve Ingoldsby | 6 + 2 musicians |

A play for 6 to 12 year olds which explores the pressures on children to fit in with their peers.
Contact: Firstcall Management, 29/30 Dame Street, Dublin 2. Tel: 01 6798401.

BEDROCK

Year	Title	Author	Cast Size
1997	Forked	Gavin Kostick	4

An exuberantly imaginative meditation on storytelling based on the legend of the blind hermaphrodite prophet, Tiresias.
Contact: Ben Hall, Curtis Brown, Haymarket House, 28/29 Haymarket, London SW1Y 4SP, England. Tel: 0171 3966600.

| 1997 | Anna's Ankle | Mark O'Rowe | 1 |

A monologue shocker about a snuff film maker.
Contact: Nick Marston at Curtis Brown, Haymarket House, 28/29 Haymarket, London SW14 4SP, England. Tel: 0171 3966600.

Year	Title	Author	Cast Size
1998	Deep Space	Alex Johnston	2

The friendship of two young Dublin men is destroyed when they both fall in love with the same woman.
Contact: Ben Hall at Curtis Brown Group Ltd., Haymarket House, 28/29 Haymarket, London SW1 4SP, England.
Tel: 0171 3966600

BELFAST THEATRE COMPANY

Year	Title	Author	Cast Size
1995	A Most Notorious Woman	Maggie Cronin	1

The life and troubled times of the Irish pirate Queen Grace O'Malley or Granuaile.

Year	Title	Author	Cast Size
1996	The Family Album of J. Edgar Hoover.	Paddy Scully	3

Hoover waits in the penthouse of an hotel in L.A. to meet Bobby Kennedy. For some reason or another the kitchen won't give him room service.

Year	Title	Author	Cast Size
1997	The Feast of Lupercal	Paddy Scully	7 + extras

A middle-aged teacher falls for a wee teenager in 1950's Belfast and almost loses his career and life.

BICKERSTAFFE THEATRE COMPANY

Year	Title	Author	Cast Size
1994	True Lines	John Crowley and Cast	4

Four Irish twenty-somethings in four parts of the world.

Year	Title	Author	Cast Size
1996	Double Helix	John Crowley and Cast	5

Irish thirty somethings finding out about how their genes have influenced their lives.

Year	Title	Author	Cast Size
1996	Hard To Believe	Conall Morrison	1

Play about coming to terms with post cease-fire Northern Ireland.
Published by: Methuen, London Tel: 0171-8408400

Year	Title	Author	Cast Size
1996	Long Black Coat	John Waters	3

Exploration of father / son relationship.
Published by: New Island Books, Dublin/Nick Hern Books, London. Tel: 01 2989937/0181 7494953.

Year	Title	Author	Cast Size
1997	Easter Dues	John Waters	4

A play about fiscal and moral corruption.

BIG TELLY THEATRE COMPANY

Year	Title	Author	Cast Size
1988	Onions	Kate Batts, Jill Holmes & Zoe Seaton	2

Thought provoking comedy about the lives of two very different bag ladies, one Catholic and one Protestant.

Year	Title	Author	Cast Size
1989	Crumbs	Kate Batts, Jill Holmes & Zoe Seaton	2

A comic two-women play set in 1798 Paris during the French Revolution.

Year	Title	Author	Cast Size
1990	Little Lucy's Magic Book	Kate Batts, Jill Holmes & Zoe Seaton	3

Lucy finds a box of tricks like no other! The contents which tumble out are not toys but the most weird and wonderful folk imaginable. For young children.

Year	Title	Author	Cast Size
1992	Twice Upon A Time	Zoe Seaton	3

Tells the legend of the highway man, Naoise O'Haughan from two different points of view. In the style of a glitzy game show.

Year	Title	Author	Cast Size
1993	I Can See The Sea	Jill Holmes & Zoe Seaton	3

A comedy, told by three local girls, telling of the hustle and bustle of a Northern Irish seaside town at the beginning of the holiday season.

Year	Title	Author	Cast Size
1995	Cuchulainn	Big Telly Theatre Co.	6

Tells the story of one of Cuchulainn's fiercest battles against the beautiful blonde Scottish chieftainess, Aoife. A battle which ultimately ends in passion.

Year	Title	Author	Cast Size
1998	To Hell With Faust	Big Telly Theatre Co.	4

A re-telling of the story of Faust from a contemporary and Irish perspective.

BLUE RAINCOAT THEATRE COMPANY

Year	Title	Author	Cast Size
1995	Vinegar Fog	Malcolm Hamilton	7

A play which deals with an individual caught up in the Salerno landings of World War II.

Year	Title	Author	Cast Size
1995	West Port Murders	Brendan Ellis	4

A play about a series of murders committed in Edinburgh, Scotland.

Year	Title	Author	Cast Size
1996	Once Time	Malcolm Hamilton	7

A play which portrays the mindscape of a man looking at his own life.

Year	Title	Author	Cast Size
1998	Still Life	Malcolm Hamilton	6

Still life tells the story of the life of French painter George Braque from the view point of Barque's wife Marcelle.

CALYPSO PRODUCTIONS

Year	Title	Author	Cast Size
1993	Hughie On The Wires	Donal O'Kelly	12

Focuses on the power and manipulation of the media and its effect on people's lives.

Year	Title	Author	Cast Size
1994	TrickleDown Town	Donal O'Kelly	4

Explores the effects of international debt and structural adjustment programmes on third world countries.

Year	Title	Author	Cast Size
1995	The Business of Blood	Donal O'Kelly	3

Tells the story of Chris Cole who made a personal and heroic stand against British Aerospace and the international arms industry.

Year	Title	Author	Cast Size
1997	Rosie and Starwars	Charlie O'Neill	6

Based on a sequence of true events, this humorous bold and tense tale explores the social exclusion of travellers in Ireland.
Contact: Charlie O'Neill, 454 South Circular Road, Dublin 8. Tel: 01 4533846.

Year	Title	Author	Cast Size
1998	Farawayan	Donal O'Kelly	10

A theatrical exploration of the experience of being unwelcomed far away from home.

CENTRE STAGE

Year	Title	Author	Cast Size
1992	The Wind and the Sleeping Harp	Roma Tomelty	2 + 2 musicians

Thomas Moore, on a return visit to Aungier Street, Dublin, reflects on his life and his Irish melodies.

Year	Title	Author	Cast Size
1992	Community Service	Roma Tomelty	4

A black comedy set in a pensioner's flat in Divis Tower. Murder, Mayhem and the Arts in West Belfast.

Year	Title	Author	Cast Size
1996	Schooled in a Foreign Voice	Roma Tomelty	3

Ulster Poets, Louis MacNeice and W.R. Rodgers meet in a Dublin pub and encounter a taciturn tinker who is not what she seems.

Year	Title	Author	Cast Size
1996	Mischief and Madness	Roma Tomelty	2 + 2 musicians

A dramatic encounter with Jonathan Swift in a hedge inn near Newry as he makes his final journey to Dublin.

CORCADORCA THEATRE COMPANY LTD.

Year	Title	Author	Cast Size
1995	Ginger Ale Boy	Enda Walsh	9

A hapless Cork ventriloquist suffers a mental breakdown at the hands of the soulless community which seems intent on crushing him.
Contact: Curtis Brown Group Ltd., Haymarket House, 28/29 Haymarket, London SW1 4SP, England. Tel: 0171 3966600.

Year	Title	Author	Cast Size
1996	Disco Pigs	Enda Walsh	2

Pig and Runt celebrate their seventeenth birthday with sad and tragic consequences.
Contact: Curtis Brown Group Ltd., Haymarket House, 28/29 Haymarket, London SW1 4SP, England. Tel: 0171 3966600.
Published by: Nick Hern Books. Tel: 0181 7494953

THE CORN EXCHANGE

Year	Title	Author	Cast Size
1995	Cultural Shrapnel	Devised by the company	6

A multi-media production consisting of five separate performances using different styles and media.

Year	Title	Author	Cast Size
1996	Streetcar	Devised by the company	4

Commedia dell'Arte version of Tennessee Williams' 'A Streetcar Named Desire'.

Year	Title	Author	Cast Size
1997	Big Bad Woolf	Devised by the company	4

Commedia dell'Arte version of Edward Albee's 'Whose Afraid of Virginia Woolf'.

Year	Title	Author	Cast Size
1997	Play On Two Chairs	Michael West	2

A fast, surprising and witty piece of physical theatre, involving two actors and two chairs.
Contact: Nick Marston at Curtis Brown, Haymarket House, 28/29 Haymarket, London SW14 4SP, England. Tel: 0171 3966600.

Year	Title	Author	Cast Size
1998	Baby Jane	Devised by the company	3

Commedia dell'Arte version of Robert Altman's film 'Whatever Happened To Baby Jane'. Deals with sister rivalry to the point of insanity.

DRUID THEATRE COMPANY

Year	Title	Author	Cast Size
1989	Wild Harvest	Ken Bourke	7

Exposes the powerlessness of a group of young men when they begin to meddle with the past and kick back against the rules which are supposed to contain them.
Contact: Ken Bourke, Quinsboro, Monasterevin, Co. Kildare. Tel: 045 525049.

Year	Title	Author	Cast Size
1990	The Donoghue Sisters	Geraldine Aron	3

Set in the attic of a family home in Ireland as the Donoghue sisters await the death of their father and talk about their unhappy lives.
Published by: Samuel French, London. Tel: 0171 3879373.

Year	Title	Author	Cast Size
1990	The Stanley Parkers	Geraldine Aron	2

A compassionate description of a relationship between two middle-aged men.

Year	Title	Author	Cast Size
1991	John Hughdy and Tom John	Vincent Woods	3

A one-act play telling the story of two men. John Hughdy is a showman who delights in shocking people. Tom John is isolated in a way his father never was.

Year	Title	Author	Cast Size
1992	Odd Habits	Marianne Fahy and Deirdre O'Kane	2

Devised from the work of Mary Lavin, this play tells the story of two novices torn between God and Brendan Bowyer.

Year	Title	Author	Cast Size
1992	At The Black Pigs Dyke	Vincent Woods	9

Set on the border between Leitrim and Fermanagh, this is the story of a community trapped in a historical cycle of violence in a time when straw people walked the roads.
Published by: Methuen, London in 'Far From The Land'. Tel: 0171 2259450.

Year	Title	Author	Cast Size
1994	Summerhouse	Robin Glendinning	5

A savagely comic and poignant study of alcoholism and family conflicts, interwoven with songs from the Church of Ireland Hymn Book.

Year	Title	Author	Cast Size
1994	Song of the Yellow Bittern	Vincent Woods	12

Explores the relevance and resonance of the past as a family comes to terms with its passions, its deaths and the unspoken laws that blind a community.

Year	Title	Author	Cast Size
1996	The Beauty Queen of Leenane	Martin McDonagh	4

The darkly comic, and ultimately tragic, tale of Maureen Folan, a plain and lonely woman in her forties, and Mag her manipulative ageing mother.
Published by: Methuen, London. Tel: 0171 8408400.
Contact: The Rod Hall Agency, 7 Goodge Place, London W1P 1FL, England. Tel: 0171 6370706.

Year	Title	Author	Cast Size
1997	Shoot the Crow	Owen McCafferty	4

The story of the bumbling petty crime efforts of four men on the make, played out through crackling dialogue and dextrous comic plotting.
Published by: Lagan Press in 'Plays and Monologues'. Distributed by Gill & McMillan. Tel: 01 4531005.

Year	Title	Author	Cast Size
1997	A Skull in Connemara	Martin McDonagh	4

Each autumn, Mick Dowd is hired to dig up enough bones in the local cemetery to make way for the new arrivals. This year strange rumours regarding his involvement in his wife's death, seven years ago, begin to emerge.
Published by: Methuen, London. Tel: 0171 8408400.
Contact: The Rod Hall Agency, 7 Goodge Place, London W1P 1FL, England. Tel: 0171 6370706.

Year	Title	Author	Cast Size
1997	The Lonesome West	Martin McDonagh	4

The story of two brothers who find it impossible to exist without the most massive and violent disputes over the most mundane and innocent of topics.
Published by: Methuen, London. Tel: 0171 8408400.
Contact: The Rod Hall Agency, 7 Goodge Place, London W1P 1FL, England. Tel: 0171 6370706.

DUBBELJOINT

Year	Title	Author	Cast Size
1994	A Night In November	Marie Jones	1

A Protestant bigot understands the nature of his own bigotry when confronted by the reality of the Greysteele bomb and

Ireland's World Cup '94 campaign.
*Published by: New Island Books, Dublin/
Nick Hern Books, London. Tel: 01 2989937/0181 7494953.*

Year	Title	Author	Cast Size
1995	Women on the Verge of HRT	Marie Jones	3 + musicians

Two middle-aged Daniel O'Donnell fans come to terms with their slipping sexuality and the invisibility of middle-age.

Year	Title	Author	Cast Size
1997	Binlids	Devised	16

Life in West Belfast from internment in 1971 through the next twenty years.

FISHAMBLE THEATRE COMPANY
(Formerly known as PIGSBACK THEATRE COMPANY)

Year	Title	Author	Cast Size
1990	Don Juan	Michael West	12

A new translation of Moliere's classic comedy about the most famously wicked womaniser ever, and how he met his nasty end.
Contact: Nick Marston at Curtis Brown, Haymarket House, 28/29 Haymarket, London SW14 4SP, England. Tel: 0171 3966600.

Year	Title	Author	Cast Size
1991	Howling Moons, Silent Sons	Deirdre Hines	8

A play set in Derry exploring how childhood fantasies become adult realities, through a series of memories and confrontations.

Year	Title	Author	Cast Size
1991	This Love Thing (co-produced with Tinderbox Theatre Company)	Marina Carr	7

A light-hearted analysis of love, as seen through the eyes of renaissance artists and some of the characters they depicted.
Contact: The Agency, 24 Pottery Lane, London W11 4LZ, England. Tel: 0171 7271346.

Year	Title	Author	Cast Size
1992	The Tender Trap	Michael West	6

An adaptation of a comedy by Marivaux, set somewhere between Hollywood and Monaco, about a prince who falls for a petrol pump attendant.
Contact: Nick Marston at Curtis Brown, Haymarket House, 28/29 Haymarket, London SW14 4SP, England. Tel: 0171 3966600.

Year	Title	Author	Cast Size
1992	The Ash Fire	Gavin Kostick	6

A compelling heart-warming saga about the first Jewish family living on the North side of Dublin in 1935.
Due to be published in 1999.
Contact: Curtis Brown, Haymarket House, 28/29 Haymarket, London SW14 4SP, England. Tel: 0171 3966600.

Year	Title	Author	Cast Size
1993	Buffalo Bill Has Gone To Alaska	Colin Teevan	6

A play set in a mythical New York inhabited by a tramplady, a newsboy, a stripper and a private eye.
Contact: Micheline Steinberg, 409 Triumph House, 187-191 Regent St., London W1R 7WF, England. Tel: 0171 2874383.

Year	Title	Author	Cast Size
1994	Jack Ketch's Gallows Jig	Gavin Kostick	6

A passionate play set in 1780, about two men and one woman in Newgate prison, waiting to be hanged.
Contact: Curtis Brown, Haymarket House, 28/29 Haymarket, London SW14 4SP, England. Tel: 0171 3966600.

Year	Title	Author	Cast Size
1995	Red Roses and Petrol	Joseph O'Connor	5

A moving and hilarious exploration of secrets, love and marriage, as a family comes together for a funeral, with explosive results.
*Published by: Methuen, London. Tel: 0171 8408400.
Contact: Blake Freidman, 122 Arlington Road, London NW1 7HP. Tel: 0171 2840408.*

\

Year	Title	Author	Cast Size
1995	Sardines	Michael West	6

A comedy of coincidences and mistaken identity, with six characters packed into a sitting room, a bedroom and a bathroom.
Contact: Nick Marston at Curtis Brown, Haymarket House, 28/29 Haymarket, London SW14 4SP, England. Tel: 0171 3966600.

Year	Title	Author	Cast Size
1996	The Flesh Addict	Gavin Kostick	6

A play about the pre-Raphaelite artists, which pulses through a gothic world of passion, obsession, delirium and death.
Contact: Curtis Brown, Haymarket House, 28/29 Haymarket, London SW14 4SP, England. Tel: 0171 3966600.

Year	Title	Author	Cast Size
1997	From Both Hips	Mark O'Rowe	6

A comic-thriller set in Dublin about a man who is accidentally shot in the hip by a garda. *Due to be published in 1999.*

Year	Title	Author	Cast Size
1998	The Nun's Wood	Pat Kinevane	6

A haunting story (set in 1974 and the present) about a secret which has been kept hidden in the wood of a County Cork convent. *Due to be published in 1999.*

FOCUS THEATRE

Year	Title	Author	Cast Size
1988	She's Your Mother Too, you know	Ena May	5

A play about the tensions that arise in a family when a mother's health deteriorates.
Contact: Society of Irish Playwrights, Irish Writers Centre, 19 Parnell Square, Dublin 1. Tel: 01 8721302.

Year	Title	Author	Cast Size
1990	Rise and Shine	Sean McCarthy	

Year	Title	Author	Cast Size
1992	Time's Up	Patrick McCabe	2

Set in prisoners visitors room against the background of the 1981 blanket protest, it tracks the deteriorating relationship of a prisioner and his girlfriend.

Year	Title	Author	Cast Size
1992	Misogynist	Michael Harding & Carmel Winters	1

A play about a man who hates women.

Year	Title	Author	Cast Size
1992	Small Box Psychosis	Barry McKinley	3

The eponymous box is a lift which breaks down, leaving a businessman at the mercy of a lift operator. *Contact: Apartment 1, 22 Pembroke Road, Dublin 4. Tel: 01 6600336*

Year	Title	Author	Cast Size
1992	Personal Ad	Paul Ryan	

Year	Title	Author	Cast Size
1997	Absent Comrades	Bill Murphy	

Absent Comrades deals with the divided loyalties of a group of Irish soldiers on the Western front. *Contact: Bill Murphy, 'Sunlodge', 65 Sunday's Well, Cork. Tel: 021 307209.*

Year	Title	Author	Cast Size
1997	Trade Me A Dream	Lindsay Jane Sedgwick	3

A thriller set against the backdrop of the troubles.
Contact: Lindsay Jane Sedgwick, 4 Strand Road, Sutton, Dublin 13. Tel: 01 8322440

Year	Title	Author	Cast Size
1997	Jack's Too Open	Paula Clamp	5

A young woman visits a family in the North of Ireland and secrets emerge.
Contact: Society of Irish Playwrights, Irish Writers Centre, 19 Parnell Square, Dublin 1. Tel: 01 8721302.

Year	Title	Author	Cast Size
1998	Healing The Dead	Johnny Hanrahan	3

Tells the story of how a woman's death engenders a family reunion and a process of healing and regeneration unfolds.
Published: Macra Na Feirme in 'Intermission Impossible'. Tel: 4508000.

YEAR	TITLE	AUTHOR	CAST SIZE
1998	Death of a Dog	Gerry O'Malley	4

A young city couple driving on a quiet road with a farmer's dog. They seek out the farmer to explain about the accident.
Contact: Gerry O'Malley, Old Conna Village, Bray, Co, Wicklow. Tel: 01 2823256

| 1998 | Him and Her | Lorcan Roche | 2 |

Is about a marriage that does not work. The man is an intellectual wimp and the woman a likeable product of an uninhibited nature.
Contact: Lorcan Roche, Ambrose, Blacklion, Greystones, Co. Wicklow. Tel: 01 2877652.

GALLOGLASS THEATRE COMPANY

YEAR	TITLE	AUTHOR	CAST SIZE
1990	The Big Sea	Colin Teevan	5

A black comedy in which three patients in a cancer ward discuss the possibility of escape.
Contact: Micheline Steinberg, 409 Triumph House, 187-191 Regent St., London W1R 7WF, England. Tel: 0171 2874383.

| 1997 | Broken Ground | Devised by the company. Scripted by Silvia Cullen. 3 |

A play which explores the push and pull of the land through three generations of women.
Contact: Silvia Cullen, The Gate Lodge, Oatlands, Glenealy, Co. Wicklow.

| 1997 | The Crack and the Whip | Colin Teevan | 7 |

A comedy with songs about lust, liquor and local politics.
Contact: Micheline Steinberg, 409 Triumph House, 187-191 Regent St., London W1R 7WF, England. Tel: 0171 2874383.

| 1998 | Breathing Space (co-production with Theatre West Glamorgan, Wales). | Devised by the company. Scripted by Ken Bourke. 8 |

Breathing space seeks to glimpse the possibility of genuine human connections in an increasingly disparate modern world.

THE GATE THEATRE

YEAR	TITLE	AUTHOR	CAST SIZE
1990	In High Germany	Dermot Bolger	1

Three young men who spent their youth on 'The Tramway End', meet in Germany but they must all return to the foreign cities in which they are forced to live.
Published by: Penguin Books in 'A Dublin Quartet'.
Tel:0171 4163000.
Contact: Nick Marston at Curtis Brown, Haymarket House, 28/29 Haymarket, London SW14 4SP, England. Tel: 0171 3966600.

| 1990 | The Tramway End | Dermot Bolger | 1 |

Consists of two plays which move through Dublin life from the 1950's to the present day. Linked by a common theme - Football.
Published by: Penguin Books in 'A Dublin Quartet'.
Tel: 0171 4163000.
Contact: Nick Marston at Curtis Brown, Haymarket House, 28/29 Haymarket, London SW14 4SP, England. Tel: 0171 3966600.

| 1994 | Molly Sweeney | Brian Friel | 3 |

A humorous, compelling drama, which tells the story of a woman who has the chance to regain her sight after being blind.
Published by: Gallery Books. Tel: 049 41779
Contact: The Agency, 24 Pottery Lane, London W11 4LZ, England. Tel: 0171 7271346.

YEAR	TITLE	AUTHOR	CAST SIZE
1996	Stella By Starlight	Bernard Farrell	6

Farrell takes a funny, wry and compassionate look at a couple coming to terms with shattered dreams, the internet and life in the Wicklow hills.
Published by: Mercier Press. Tel: 021 275040.
Contact: Rosica Colin Ltd., 1, Clareville Grove Mews, London SW7 5AH, England. Tel: 0171 3701080

| 1997 | The Weeping of Angels | Joseph O'Connor | 6 |

Set in the not too distant future, the three last nuns in Dublin encounter two workmen. As Christmas Eve dawns fate is about to intervene with hilarious results.
Contact: Blake Freidman, 122 Arlington Road, London NW1 7HP. Tel: 0171 2840408.

| 1998 | The Weir | Conor McPherson | 5 |

On arriving at a small country bar, Valerie finds herself spellbound by an evening of ghostly stories from the area's bachelors.
Published by: Nick Hern Books (in association with Royal Court).
Tel: 0181 7494953.
Contact: Nick Marston, Curtis Browne Ltd., Haymarket House, 28-29 Haymarket, London SW1Y 4SP, England. Tel: 0171 3966600

GRAFFITI THEATRE COMPANY

YEAR	TITLE	AUTHOR	CAST SIZE
1989	White Heat	Roger Gregg	3

A senior cycle theatre in education programme dealing with the effects of apartheid.

| 1989 | Messer | Graffiti Theatre Company | 2 |

A primary school programme on environmental awareness.

| 1991 | Infidel | Roger Gregg | 4 |

A senior cycle theatre in education programme concerning the cause and effect of religious warfare.

| 1992 | You Can't Talk About That On Jo-Maxi | Graffiti Theatre Company | 3 |

A post primary programme that examines the thought control which surrounds adolescents.

| 1992 | The Dogs of Chulainn | Roger Gregg | 4 |

A production which examines the fate of three soldiers in the United States army on the night before Custer's last stand.

| 1993 | Fishy Tales | Enda Walsh | 3 |

A story of an arrogant prince who is being punished for his bad behaviour and is sent on a journey.

| 1994 | Crossing The Boundary | Roger Gregg | 4 |

Set in the afterlife the play examines the clash between Celtic individualism and the roman desire to systematise society.

YEAR	TITLE	AUTHOR	CAST SIZE
1997	Forget Me Not	Graffiti Theatre Company	3

Primary programme centred around the dramatic telling of three fantastical stories.

| 1998 | The Changeling | Graffiti Theatre Company | 4 |

A programme for primary schools dealing with substance misuse.

ISLAND THEATRE COMPANY

Year	Title	Author	Cast Size
1992	The Crunch	Mike Finn and Terry Devlin	8

A free adaptation of Moliere's 'Tartuffe'.

Year	Title	Author	Cast Size
1995	Charlie Chaplin's Mother was an Irishman.	Mike Finn and Terry Devlin	1

The story of one night in the life of a Limerick man - and the actor who plays him.

| 1996 | The Ante Room | Kevin O'Connor | 9 |

An adaptation of the novel by Kate O'Brien.
Contact: Kevin O'Connor, 52 Edendale Road, Ranelagh, Dublin 6.

| 1998 | Borrowed Robes | John Barrett | 6 |

Set against the background of 'the Limerick Pogrom' this play explores the possible motivations of the main protagonists.
Contact: John Barrett, 29 Saval Park Gardens, Dalkey, Co. Dublin.

KABOSH PRODUCTIONS

Year	Title	Author	Cast Size
1994	Macbeth the Musical	Paul Boyd	8

Musical work of Shakespeare's infamous play. A comic interpretation with a musical edge.

| 1996 | Freefalling | Owen McCafferty | 2 |

Two joyriders get caught up in fantasy which delivers drastic consequences in reality.
Published by: Lagan Press in 'Plays and Monologues'.
Distributed by Gill & McMillan. Tel: 01 4531005.
Contact: Owen McCafferty, 18 Glendale Park, Belfast BT8.
Tel: 01232 298382.

| 1998 | Mojo - Mickybo | Owen McCafferty | 2 |

Two Belfast children live in a world of cinematic dreams until a killing brings violence into their world.
Published by: Lagan Press. Distributed by Gill & McMillan.
Tel: 01 4531005.
Contact: Owen McCafferty, 18 Glendale Park, Belfast BT8. Tel: 01232 298382.

LYRIC THEATRE, BELFAST

Year	Title	Author	Cast Size
1988	Culture Vultures	Robin Glendinning	

Play exploring the survival or otherwise, of the idealism of three young Northern Ireland people.

| 1989 | The Belle of Belfast City | Christina Reid | 8 |

The story of three generations of a Northern Irish family.

| 1989 | Charlie Gorilla | John McClelland | 9 |

Powerful play about a zookeeper's attempts to breed gorillas for commercial purposes.

Year	Title	Author	Cast Size
1991	Rough Beginnings	Robert Ellison	

The hopes, dreams and traumas of a group of Belfast teenagers.

| 1991 | Pygmies In The Ruins | Ron Hutchinson | 11 (plus children) |

Play confronting Ireland's attitude to its own past through the experience of a police 'Scene of Crime' photographer.

| 1992 | Round The Big Clock | John Boyd | |

A whistle-stop history of Belfast.

Year	Title	Author	Cast Size
1993	Put Out That Light	Theresa Donnelly	9

The story of a Falls Road family during the Belfast blitz during World War II.

| 1993 | How Many Miles to Babylon | Jennifer Johnston | 6 |

Poignant story of childhood friends separated by culture and class who as young men, serve together in World War I.

| 1994 | Galloping Buck Jones (co-production with Tinderbox Theatre Company) | Ken Bourke | 5 |

A swaggering romp, set 200 years ago, along the notorious Belfast/Dublin highway.
Contact: Ken Bourke, Quinsboro, Monasterevin, Co. Kildare.
Tel: 045-525049.

| 1994 | Pictures of Tomorrow (co-produced with Point Fields) | Martin Lynch | 7 |

Three companions recall shared memories of the Spanish Civil War.

| 1994 | A Private Picture Show | Owen McCafferty | |

Adult play about a writer who cannot make himself write.
Contact: Owen McCafferty, 18 Glendale Park, Belfast BT8.
Tel: 01232 298382.
Published by: Lagan Press in 'Plays and Monologues'.
Distributed by Gill & McMillan. Tel: 01 4531005.

| 1995 | Lengthening Shadows (Co-produced with Point Fields) | Graham Reid | 5 |

A powerful portrait, both of a family and of the dramatic times they've lived through.

| 1996 | Drive On! | Bill Morrison | 6 |

Adult comedy about a man reliving his past lives and loves, as he faces selling the family home.

| 1996 | The Desert Lullaby | Jennifer Johnston | 5 |

Two women reflect on a moment exactly fifty years ago which has shaped every second of their lives since.

| 1998 | Tearing The Loom | Gary Mitchell | 7 |

Drama centred on one family divided on the two sides of the 1798 rebellion.
Published by: Nick Hern Books, London. Tel: 0181 7494953.

THE MACHINE

Year	Title	Author	Cast Size
1996	The Yellow Man	Michael Scott and Brian Thunder	3 +2 musicians

Adapted from the artist Pauline Bewick's tale.

| 1996 | The Cuchulain Cycle | Michael Scott | 8 |

Musical adaptation of W.B. Yeats' play.

| 1997 | Dracula | Michael Scott | 8 |

Adaptation of Bram Stoker's gothic and timeless tale.

| 1998 | Purgatory | Michael Scott | 4 |

Opera adaptation of W.B. Yeats' play.

MACNAS

Year	Title	Author	Cast Size
1992	Táin	Adapted by Páraic Breathnach and devised by the company	12

Cúchullainn engages in the defence of Ulster from the covetous Queen Medb of Connaught.

| 1994 | Buile Shuibhne/Sweeny | Adapted by Páraic Breathnach and devised by the company | 10 |

King Sweeny is cursed by an abbot and descends into madness.

| 1995 | Balor | Adapted by Páraic Breathnach and devised by the company | 10 |

Balor, a Celtic cyclops, rules Tory Island with a terrible power, but his fate is sealed in a Druid's prophecy.

| 1996 | Rhymes From The Ancient Mariner | Rod Goodall & Patricia Ford and devised by the company | 16 |

A promenade production of Coleridge's poem.

| 1998 | The Dead School | Patrick McCabe | 6 |

Raphael Bell, old style teacher, has his class rehearse his life.

| 1998 | Diamonds In The Soil | Patrick O'Reilly and devised by the company | 11 |

A highly visual show inspired by the life and work of Vincent Van Gogh.

MERIDIAN THEATRE COMPANY

Year	Title	Author	Cast Size
1989	The Overcoat	Johnny Hanrahan	5

A musical adaptation of Gogol's classic tale set in Tsarist Russia and centring on a dim witted clerk's search for transcendence through the acquisition of a 'magical overcoat'.

| 1989 | The School For Wives | Derek Mahon | 6 |

Light hearted verse update of Moliere's classic Comedy of Manners. Published by: Gallery Press. Tel: 049 41779.

| 1994 | The Art of Waiting | Johnny Hanrahan | 6 |

A play examining family history and relationships in the upper-middle-class setting of a large established family hotel in a small Irish town.

| 1997 | Reading Turgenev | Johnny Hanrahan | 6 |

An ensemble staging of William Trevor's masterly depiction of small town stagnation and a young woman's obsessive romantic quest to transcend it. Published by: Meridian / Collins Press. Tel: 021 506522.

| 1998 | Craving | Johnny Hanrahan and John Browne | 4 |

Music theatre piece using film by Alan Gilsenan, examining the worlds of advertising, media and designer lifestyle.

THE NATIONAL THEATRE SOCIETY LTD
(For further information on all plays, please contact the Abbey Theatre)

Year	Title	Author	Cast Size
1988	Summer	Hugh Leonard	8

Published by: Colin Smythe, 1991. Tel: 01753 886000.

Year	Title	Author	Cast Size
1988	Exit Entrance	Aidan C. Matthews	4
1988	Times In It	Frank McGuinness	
1988	A Trinity of Two	Ulick O'Connor	2
1988	Josephine In The Night	Aodhan Madden	1
1988	Dark Lady	Karen Sunde	12
1988	O Ananias, Azarias and Misael	Jennifer Johnston	1
1998	Snow White	Tom McIntyre	7
1988	Boss Grady's Boys	Sebastian Barry	8

Contact: The Agency, 24 Pottery Lane, London W11 4LZ, England. Tel: 0171 7271346.

1989	Blood Guilty	Antoine Ó Flatharta	4
1989	Goodbye Carraroe	Neil Donnelly	3
1989	The Reel McCoy	Neil Donnelly	14
1989	Too Late for Logic	Tom Murphy	18

Contact: Alexandra Cann, 12a Abingdon Road, London W8 6AS, England. Tel: 0171 9384002.

1989	Triptych	Jennifer Johnston	3
1989	Una Pooka	Michael Harding	7
1989	Shades of the Jellywoman	Peter Sheridan and Jean Doyle	1
1990	Misogynist	Michael Harding	15
1990	Blinded by the Light	Dermot Bolger	13

Published by: Nick Hern Books. Tel: 0171 7462046.
Contact: Nick Marston, Curtis Brown Group Ltd., Haymarket House, 28 - 29 Haymarket, London SW1Y 4SP, England. Tel:

1990	Frauds	Fergus Linehan	8
1990	Kitty O'Shea	Tom McIntyre	2
1990	Mamie Sighs	Donal O'Kelly	1

Contact: Alexandra Cann, 12a Abingdon Road, London W8 6AS, England. Tel: 0171 9384002.

| 1990 | Prayers of Sherkin | Sebastian Barry | 12 |

Published by: Methuen, London. Tel: 0171 2259450.

| 1991 | The Gigli Concert | Tom Murphy | 3 |

Contact: Alexandra Cann, 12a Abingdon Road, London W8 6AS, England. Tel: 0171 9384002.

| 1991 | The Murphy Initiative | Niall Williams | 7 |
| 1991 | The Power of Darkness | John McGahern | 7 |

Published by: Faber & Faber, London. Tel: 0171 4650045

| 1991 | Danny, The Witch & The Goblin | Alan Cullen | 10 |
| 1991 | Ullaloo | Marina Carr | 2 |

Contact: The Agency, 24 Pottery Lane, London W11 4LZ, England. Tel: 0171 7271346.

| 1991 | The Lament For Arthur Cleary | Dermot Bolger | 5 |

Contact: Nick Marston at Curtis Brown, Haymarket House, 28/29 Haymarket, London SW14 4SP, England. Tel: 0171 3966600.

| 1991 | One Last White Horse | Dermot Bolger | 9 |

Contact: Nick Marston at Curtis Brown, Haymarket House, 28/29 Haymarket, London SW14 4SP, England. Tel: 0171 3966600.

| 1992 | Moving | Hugh Leonard | 9 |

Published by: French Acting, 1994.

| 1992 | Away Alone | Janet Noble | 8 |

YEAR	TITLE	AUTHOR	CAST SIZE
1992	White Woman Street	Sebastian Barry	6

Contact: The Agency, 24 Pottery Lane, London W11 4LZ, England. Tel: 0171 7271346.

| 1992 | Silverlands | Antoine Ó Flatharta | 10 |
| 1993 | Someone Who'll Watch Over Me | Frank McGuinness | 3 |

Published by: Faber & Faber, London. Tel: 0171 4650045

| 1993 | The Last Apache Reunion | Bernard Farrell | 8 |

Published by: Mercier Press. Tel: 021 275040.

| 1993 | Wonderful Tennessee | Brian Friel | 6 |

Published by: Faber & Faber, London. Tel: 0171 4650045.

| 1993 | Hubert Murray's Widow | Michael Harding | 8 |
| 1993 | Euripides' 'The Trojan Women' | Brian Kennelley | 11 |

New version.
Published by: Bloodaxe Books, 1993. Tel: 01434 240500.

| 1993 | The Cavalcaders | Billy Roche | 6 |

Contact: The Agency, 24 Pottery Lane, London W11 4LZ, England. Tel: 0171 7271346.

| 1993 | Brothers Of The Bush | Jimmy Murphy | 4 |

Published by: Oberon Books, 1994, London. Tel: 0171 6073637.

1994	The Bird Sanctuary	Frank McGuinness	5
1994	Chamber Music	Hugh Leonard	8
1994	Sheep's Milk On The Boil	Tom Mac Intyre	13

Published by: Dedalus Press. Tel: 01 4902582.

| 1994 | The Broken Jug | John Banville | 11 |

After Kleist.
Published by: Gallery Books. 049 41779.

| 1994 | Asylum! Asylum! | Donal O'Kelly | 6 |

Published by: Syracuse University Press in 'New Plays From The Abbey Theatre'.
Contact: Alexandra Cann, 12a Abingdon Road, London W8 6AS, England. Tel: 0171 9384002.

| 1994 | The Mai | Marina Carr | 8 |

Published by: Gallery Press, 1995. Tel: 049 41779.
Contact: The Agency, 24 Pottery Lane, London W11 4LZ, England. Tel: 0171 7271346.

| 1995 | The Only True History of Lizzie Finn | Sebastian Barry | 17 |

Published by: Methuen, London, 1995. Tel: 0171 8408400.

1995	The Duty Master	Neil Donnelly	15
1995	Small City	Clare Dowling	
1995	Vinegar and Brown Paper	Colin Teevan	3

Contact: Micheline Steinberg, 409 Triumph House, 187-191 Regent St., London W1R 7WF, England. Tel: 0171 2874383.

YEAR	TITLE	AUTHOR	CAST SIZE
1995	The Third Law of Motion	Brian Lynch	
1995	April Bright	Dermot Bolger	7

Published by: New Island Books, Dublin/Nick Hern Books, London, 1997. Tel: 01 2989937/0181 7494953.

YEAR	TITLE	AUTHOR	CAST SIZE
1995	Play Girl	Katy Hayes	3
1995	Monkey	Michael West	3

Contact: Nick Marston at Curtis Brown, Haymarket House, 28/29 Haymarket, London SW14 4SP, England. Tel: 0171 3966600.

| 1996 | The Adventures of Shay Mouse | Pat McCabe | 10 |

Published by: New Island Books, Dublin/Nick Hern Books, London, 1997. Tel: 01 2989937/0181 7494953.

| 1996 | The Invisible Mending Company | Philip Davison | 10 |
| 1996 | She Stoops To Folly | Adapted by Tom Murphy | 24 |

After 'The Vicar of Wakefield'

| 1996 | The Marriage of Figaro | Michael West | 16 |

A new version of Beaumarchais's classic.
Contact: Nick Marston at Curtis Brown, Haymarket House, 28/29 Haymarket, London SW14 4SP, England. Tel: 0171 3966600.

| 1996 | Portia Coughlan | Marina Carr | 12 |

Published by: Faber & Faber, London, 1996. 0171 4650045.
Contact: The Agency, 24 Pottery Lane, London W11 4LZ, England. Tel: 0171 7271346.

| 1996 | Good Evening, Mr. Collins | Tom Mac Intyre | 9 |

Published by: Faber & Faber, London. Tel: 0171 4650045.

| 1996 | Strawberries in December | Antoine Ó Flatharta | 28 |

Presented by the National Youth Theatre.

| 1996 | Cré na Cille | Máirtín Ó Cadhain | 9 |
| 1997 | In A Little World Of Our Own | Gary Mitchell | 5 |

Published by: Nick Hern Books, London. Tel: 0181 7494953.

1997	Sour Grapes	Michael Harding	8
1997	The Chirpaun	Tom Mac Intyre	7
1997	A Picture of Paradise	Jimmy Murphy	

Published by: Faber & Faber, London. Tel: 0171 4650045.

| 1997 | Melonfarmer | Alex Johnston | 8 |
| 1997 | Give Me Your Answer, Do! | Brian Friel | 9 |

Published by: Penguin Books, London, 1997. 0171 416300.

| 1997 | Tarry Flynn | Conall Morrison | 29 |

A new adaptation of Patrick Kavanagh's novel.

| 1997 | The Secret Fall of Constance Wilde | Tom Kilroy | 9 |

Published by: The Gallery Press, 1997. 049 41779.

1997	Respond	Noel MacAoidh	
1997	The Papar	Brian Fitzgibbon	
1997	A Different Rhyme	Lorraine O'Brien	
1998	The Wake	Tom Murphy	11

Published by: Methuen, London. Tel: 0171 8408400

| 1998 | Kevin's Bed | Bernard Farrell | 12 |

YEAR	TITLE	AUTHOR	CAST SIZE
1998	Swans, Boots and Boxes	Eugene McCabe, Eilis Ní Dhuibhne & Dermot Healy	

Year	Title	Author	Cast Size
1998	Twenty Grand	Declan Hughes	6

Published by: Methuen, London in 'Hughes, Plays One'.
Tel: 0171 8408400
Contact: Nick Marston at Curtis Brown, Haymarket House, 28/29
Haymarket, London SW14 4SP, England. Tel: 0171 3966600.

1998	As The Beast Sleeps	Gary Mitchell	7
1998	Caoineadh Airt Ui Laoghaire	Tom Mac Intyre	10
1998	The Electrocution of Children	Chris Lee	9
1998	At Swim Two Birds	Alex Johnson	

A new adaptation of Flann O'Brien's novel.

1998	Amazing Grace	Michael Harding	
1998	By The Bog Of Cats	Marina Carr	15

Published by: Gallery Press. Tel: 04941779.

PAN PAN THEATRE COMPANY

Year	Title	Author	Cast Size
1994	Martin Assassin Of His Wife	Gavin Quinn & Stephen Walsh	5

A love story.

1995	Mademoiselle Hic Hac in the Red Room	Gavin Quinn	8

An adaptation from the Damascus Plays by August Strindberg.

1995	A Bronze Twist of Your Serpent Muscles	Gavin Quinn	2

A play about madness.

1996	Tailors Requiem	Gavin Quinn	4

A master tailor binds his apprentices to endless work. Their only escape is into a world of their own.

1997	Peepshow	Gavin Quinn	4

Secret and pathetic lives of Amy, George, Paddy and Selina all living close together in a small neighbourhood.

1998	Cartoon	Gavin Quinn	2

An adaptation of Andreas Staudinger's political satire based on the life and career of Benito Mussolini.

THE PASSION MACHINE THEATRE COMPANY

Year	Title	Author	Cast Size
1988	Going Places	Aidan Parkinson	8

A drama about CIE workers, written and directed by a one time bus conductor.
Published by: Passion Machine Theatre Company.
Tel: 01 8788857.

1988	Breaking Up	Brendan Gleeson	18

Deals with a group of lads who have just left school and are looking forward to a last summer together, having to deal with the realities of adulthood.
Published by: Passion Machine Theatre Company.
Tel: 01 8788857.

1988	Home	Paul Mercier	10

A play about Michael from Westmeath, who has migrated to Dublin to his first bedsit. Looking for work is the least of his worries, as he finds that coping with his neighbourhood is work enough for him.
Published by: Passion Machine Theatre Company.
Tel: 01 8788857.

1989	War	Roddy Doyle	16

A comedy about a fight to the death, between two rival teams at a charity pub quiz.

1993	Pilgrims	Paul Mercier	9

A beach in the South-West of Ireland is the tale for an intersection through a series of encounters between nine people, four couples and a solitary beachcomber.

1994	Melting Penguins	Gerard Stembridge	5

A play about five penguins waddling their way into the mysteries of the depletion of the Ozone layer.

1994	The Man Who Cared Too Much	Frank Shouldice	6

A play about an arrogant TV host, his sycophantic assistant and their show.

1994	The Last Potato	Joe O'Byrne	6

A band of famine survivors have to decide what to do with a rare potato and a captured young man they refer to as it.

1994	Sheep, Shite and Desolation	Nell McCaffery	1

An amusing tribute to the Irish Countrywomen's association and one of its members who campaigns for modern comforts in place of rural deprivations.

1994	Where The Heart Is	Michael Harding	1

A story of a lonely old man who has been travelling the road with a cardboard box containing his mother's dinner service.

1994	Babies and Bathwater	Brendan Gleeson	2

A play about two men, one who does not care about the environment and the other desperately anxious about the world in which he is raising his children.

1994	Between Venus and Mars	Antoine Ó Flatharta	1

A play about the loneliness and desperation of the human spirit, one man sacrificing himself for the good of mankind.

1994	Ghost Acreage At Vixen Time	Deirdre Anne Hines	6

A young farmer and his wife struggle against the loss of the pastoral vision and its practical adjuncts.

1994	Love Machines	Johnny Hanrahan	5

A play set in a technical world where people never meet each other, as they communicate on modern gadgets.

1994	Dectire	John McArdle	9

A play centred on the birth of Setanta and its harmonic symbolism for the world.

1995	Too Much Too Young	Anto Nolan	3

A play about three men in their late twenties who fulfill a vow to reunite on the anniversary of the first Madness concert ever staged in Ireland.

1995	Buddleia	Paul Mercier	28

A fable about modern Dublin, an offbeat and episodic depiction of city life.

1996	Kitchensink	Paul Mercier	4

A little history of suburbia in the form of a surreal, comic and poetic tale spanning a period of three decades.

1997	Massive Damages	Declan Lynch	7

A play that deals with such contemporary concerns as the law, the media, show business and deformation of character.

1998   Fully Recovered   Anto Nolan   9
A play about a group of men, working out a nine to five existence in a Dublin sweatshop, through backstabbing, gossip and petty power games.

PROJECT ARTS CENTRE

Year	Title	Author	Cast Size
1993	Foggy Hair and Green Eyes	Tom Mac Intyre	1

One man show - performed in bedroom No 47 of the Clarence Hotel duration 25 minutes.

1993   Lipstick on the Host   Caroline Fitzgerald
**   and Colette Proctor   1**
A one woman show adapted from the work of Aidan Mathews which tells the story of a forty-something teacher who falls in love and breaks taboos.

1993   Twinkle Toes   Jennifer Johnson   1
The story of the wife of a Republican paramilitary who has been in prison for nine years and is desperately aware that the best years of her life are being wasted.

1993   The Stronger   Frank McGuinness   3
Translation of Strindberg's work. A meeting between two women in a cafe on Christmas Eve who become involved in a conversation with a stranger - with life or death consequences.

1993   The man with the
**   flower in his mouth   Frank McGuinness   3**
A new translation of Pirandello's play about a man killing time in an all-night cafe on Christmas Eve, who becomes involved in a conversation with a stranger.

1993   Tyrannosaurus Twerp   Maeve Ingoldsby   5
Delightful play for children young (6) and old (60). The adventures of a young lovable, lost Tyrannosaurus in his journey to find his home and safety. *Contact: Firstcall Management, 29/30 Dame Street, Dublin 2. Tel: 01 6798401.*

1994   Big Mom   Ferdia McAnna   4
A play with music which follows an ageing country music star as she surrounds herself with her beautiful daughters for the comeback tour.

1994   The Kiss   Michael Harding   1
The story of a lonely and deeply disturbed priest incarcerated for sex-crimes.

1994   Seachange   John Banville   2
A man with no memory and a woman with only painful memories meet for a moment.

1994   Greatest Hits   Thomas McLaughlin   2
"The most harrowing, brutal and obscene piece of work to come out of what we euphemistically call The Troubles in Northern Ireland." Sunday Independent
Published by: New Island Books, Dublin/Nick Hern Books, London. Tel: 01 2989937/0181 7494953.

1994   The Marlboro Man   Clare Dowling   3
Disturbing exploration of a relationship in contemporary Ireland. A young couple confront their ghosts in the confines of the married quarters of an army barracks.
Published by: New Island Books, Dublin/Nick Hern Books, London. Tel: 01 2989937/0181 7494953.

1995   Troubled Hearts   Jim Culleton   4
Adapted from three short stories by Maeve Binchy, Troubled Hearts tells three bittersweet stories of life, lust and the adventures in between.

1996   The Gay Detective   Gerard Stembridge   7
The Gay Detective tells the story of a brilliant young Garda Sergeant based in Dublin who is homosexual. The play traces the impact of contemporary Ireland on his views and beliefs.
Published by: New Island Books, Dublin/Nick Hern Books, London. Tel: 01 2989937/0181 7494953.

RED KETTLE THEATRE COMPANY

Year	Title	Author	Cast Size
1991	Moonshine	Jim Nolan	6

Easter. A seaside town. Against all odds a madcap undertaker tries to stage a version of A Midsummer Nights Dream.
Published by: Gallery Press. Tel: 049 41779.

1992   Forty-Four Sycamore   Bernard Farrell   5
A 'new' middle-class couple try to impress and entertain more established neighbours, with hilarious results.
Published by: Mercier Press. Tel: 021 275040.

1993   Chickadee   Tom Mac Intyre   9
The older man, the younger girl, her parents desperate and helpless. A comedy of male sexual terror.

1994   The Guernica Hotel   Jim Nolan   6
A Spanish Civil War veteran of the international brigade struggles to come to terms with the politics of modern Ireland.
Contact: The Agency, 24 Pottery Lane, London W11 4LZ, England. Tel: 0171 7271346.

1994   Happy Birthday
**   Dear Alice   Bernard Farrell   6**
An elderly but defiant Alice hilariously resists her family's attempts to consign her to a nursing home.
Published by: Mercier Press. Tel: 021 275040.
Contact: Rosica Colin Ltd., 1 Charleville Grove Mews, London SW7 5AH, England. Tel: 0171 3701080.

1995   Backsides to the Wind   Michael Harding   8
A small town is turned on its head by the imminent arrival of The President.

1995   Catalpa - The Movie   Donal O'Kelly   1
A failed screenwriter is obsessed with his life's dream - making Catalpa - The movie. An extraordinary act of theatre.
Published by: New Island Books, Dublin/Nick Hern Books, London. Tel: 01 2989937/0181 7494953.
Contact: Alexandra Cann, 12a Abingdon Road, London W8 6AS, England. Tel: 0171 9384002.

1997   The Stomping Ground   Loughlin Deegan   8
A group of college students gather in a small town for a booze soaked weekend, but the events of a year before threaten to spoil the party.
Contact: The Rod Hall Agency, 7 Goodge Place, London W1P 1FL, England. Tel: 0171 6370706.

1998   The Salvage Shop   Jim Nolan   6
Alcoholic bandmaster, Sylvie Tansay is haunted by personal betrayal. As the band moves to unseat him, his son evokes the intervention of Luciano Pavarotti.
Published by: Gallery Press. Tel: 049 41779.
Contact: The Agency, 24 Pottery Lane, London W11 4LZ, England. Tel: 0171 7271346.

REPLAY PRODUCTIONS

Year	Title	Author	Cast Size
1988	Under Napoleon's Nose	Marie Jones	6

A theatre in education play for secondary schools.

1994   Hidden Charges   Arthur Riordan   4

A visit from Auntie Kitty is the last thing a troubled relationship needs. The power of euphemisms and secrets is exploited to deadly effect by the sinister handyman.
Published by: To be published in 1999 by New Island Books in 'Rough Magic - First Plays' Tel: 01 2989937.

1995   Danti-Dan   Gina Moxley   5

Cork 1970, summer holidays, kids going crazy with heat, boredom and frustration, and in the giddy atmosphere sex is the great mystery to be explored.
Published by: Faber & Faber, London in 'The Dazzling Dark (New Irish Plays)'. Tel: 0171 4650045.
also to be published in 1999 by New Island Books in 'Rough Magic - First Plays'. Tel: 01 2989937.
Contact: Alexandra Cann, 12a Abingdon Road, London W8 6AS, England. Tel: 0171 9384002.

1997   Halloween Night   Declan Hughes   10

In an apocalyptic test of faith a welcome-home party turns to nightmare when the supernatural appears to invade a house cut off by sea.
Published by: Methuen, London in 'Hughes, Plays One'. Tel: 0171 8408400
Contact: Nick Marston at Curtis Brown, Haymarket House, 28/29 Haymarket, London SW14 4SP, England. Tel: 0171 3966600.

1997   Mrs. Sweeney   Paula Meehan   6

As Lil attempts to come to terms with their daughter's death her husband starts to behave like a pigeon. A study of madness in an insane world.
Published by: To be published in 1999 by New Island Books in 'Rough Magic - First Plays'. Tel: 01 2989937.

STORYTELLERS THEATRE COMPANY

YEAR	TITLE	AUTHOR	CAST SIZE
1989	The Trial of Esther Waters	Mary Elizabeth Burke-Kennedy	6

In a story teaming with Victorian life, Esther Waters fights to bring up her child against all the forces of society and convention.

1993	Silas Marner	Mary Elizabeth Burke-Kennedy	6

This adaptation finds a lively contemporary theatrical idiom for a timeless fable of fate, destiny and faith.

1995	Emma	Mary Elizabeth Burke-Kennedy	8

Jane Austen's irony is perfectly contained in this witty and vigorous adaptation which presents the heroine in all her infuriating and lovable complexity.

YEAR	TITLE	AUTHOR	CAST SIZE
1996	Wuthering Heights	Mary Elizabeth Burke-Kennedy	7

Heathcliff and Cathy's epic love story is told in the context of a folk tale of two generations of Earnshaws and Lintons.

1998	Hard Times	Mary Elizabeth Burke-Kennedy	7

This taut adaptation skilfully weaves the stories of the Gradgrinds and Stephen Blackpool, and highlights the central necessity for the arts in human development.

1998	When the Wall Came Down	Renate Ahrens-Kramer	4

When the wall came down is a powerful piece of theatre exploring one of the personal dilemmas experienced by many after the fall of the Berlin wall.
Contact: Renate Ahrens-Kramer, 'Rockingham', Nerano Road, Dalkey, Do. Dublin. Tel: 01 2859113.

TEAM EDUCATIONAL THEATRE COMPANY

YEAR	TITLE	AUTHOR	CAST SIZE
1988	Dear Kenny	Jim Nolan	3-5

Focuses on the process of ageing and deals with the concerns of pre-teens. *Contact: The Agency, 24 Pottery Lane, London W11 4LZ, England. Tel: 0171 7271346.*

1989	The Native Ground	Antoine Ó Flatharta	3-5

Exploration of the cautious interaction between some members of the travelling and settled communities.

1989	Dreamwalker	John McArdle	3-5

Exploration of the role and importance of imagination and creativity.

1990	Ambrose and the Gumbleuhumps	Roger Cregg	3-5

Explores and stimulates an awareness of music and musicality.

1990	Shadowtackle	Anne Barrett	3-5

Exploration of the choices and decisions that confront young people in the transition between school and the world beyond.

1991	Firestone	Maeve Ingoldsby	3-5

Exploration of the balance of nature using the four elements to examine the physical world and how it works.
Contact: Firstcall Management, 29/30 Dame Street, Dublin 2. Tel: 01 6798401.

1991	Performers	John McArdle	3-5

Exploration of the search for spiritual values in the post-modern world.

1992	Earwigs	Maeve Ingoldsby	3-5

Explores the complex relationships between adults and 11/12 year olds.
Contact: Firstcall Management, 29/30 Dame Street, Dublin 2. Tel: 01 6798401.

1992	Here Come Cowboys	Colin Teevan	3-5

Explores the games people play, how young people exploit each other, peer pressure and isolation.
Contact: Micheline Steinberg, 409 Triumph House, 187-191 Regent St., London W1R 7WF, England. Tel: 0171 2874383.

1993	One Star Away	Sean Moffat	3-5

Examines how children cope with emotional problems and explore opportunities of expressing themselves in stressful situations.

1993	The Well	Ken Bourke	3-5

Explores consequences for relationships within a family when significant matters remain unacknowledged and undiscussed.
Contact: Ken Bourke, Quinsboro, Monasterevin, Co. Kildare. Tel: 045-525049.

1994	Monkey Puzzle Tree	Maeve Ingoldsby	3-5

A play about different attitudes and approaches to dealing with the tasks and challenges of everyday life. *Contact: Firstcall Management, 29/30 Dame Street, Dublin 2. Tel: 01 6798401.*

1994	Out of Line	Maeve Ingoldsby	3-5

Deals with the changing concepts and patterns of work and their effects on the life choices people make. *Contact: Firstcall Management, 29/30 Dame Street, Dublin 2. Tel: 01 6798401.*

1995	Kirkle	Paula Meehan	4

Focuses on the child's exploration of the world of sound with its patterns and rhythms and language in various forms.

1995	Fixing Bill Haley	Ken Bourke	4

Encourages people to consider work in a holistic way. Explores different value systems to work.

Year	Title	Author	Cast Size
1996	Two Houses	John McArdle	4

Explores the concepts of truth, justice and the law, set in pre-famine Ireland.

Year	Title	Author	Cast Size
1996	Black Ice	Thomas McLoughlin	5

Explores the issues surrounding young people leaving home and homelessness.

1997	The Voyage	Paula Meehan	5

Explores the themes of home, exile, loss and leave-taking, loneliness and friendship, trust and deceit.

1998	Silly Millie's Storybook	John McArdle	4

Focuses on children's experience of feelings, their ability to recognise emotions and to express and share these feelings.

1998	Shoot the Butterfly	Thomas McLoughlin	5

Explores identity and self-definition at times of transition in life.

THEATRE OMNIBUS

Year	Title	Author	Cast Size
1990	Brian Boru	Michael Harding	50-200

The wake and funeral of Brian Boru. 'An exploration of the Irish hero'.

1992	Last Night's Fun	Dermot Healy	3

An exploration of sound as language between a couple and their mother-in-law.

1997	The Spell of The Mega Mall	Max Hafler (advisory writer)	30

Multi-media play with disabled and ablebodied actors and performers on the subject of supermarkets, cloning, progress etc.

TINDERBOX THEATRE COMPANY

Year	Title	Author	Cast Size
1989	Theatre of Paranoia	Miche Doherty	3

Young man's worst nightmare comes true.

1989	Fingertips	Thomas McLoughlin	5

Young man interrogated in Belfast.

1991	This Love Thing (co-produced with Pigs Back Theatre Company)	Marina Carr	7

Witty exploration of love through the ages. *Contact: The Agency, 24 Pottery Lane, London W11 4LZ, England. Tel: 0171 7271346.*

1993	Independent Voice	Gary Mitchell	5

Two journalists from a community newspaper in Belfast struggle to tell the truth.

1994	Galloping Buck Jones (co-produced with The Lyric Theatre)	Ken Bourke	5

Outrageous romp set in the late 1700's on the life of Frederick Jones, theatre lover and pursuer of highway men.

1996	Language Roulette	Daragh Carville	6

An explosive re-union in a pub on 'pound a pint' night during the first cease-fire in Belfast. *Published by: Methuen, London in 'Far From The Land'. Tel: 0171 8408400. Contact: Casarotto Ramsay Ltd., National House, 60-66 Wardour Street, London SIV 4ND, England. Tel: 0171 2874450.*

Year	Title	Author	Cast Size
1997	Dumped	Daragh Carville	5

'Dumped' stand-up comedian, living in a skip, enlists the help of two 'skip hokers' to get his girlfriend back. *Published by: Tinderbox Theatre Company. Tel: 01232 439313. Contact: Casarotto Ramsay Ltd., National House, 60-66 Wardour Street, London WIV 4ND, England. Tel: 0171 2874450.*

1998	Into the Heartland	John McClelland	4

Sligo man. now retired in Whitehead, assesses his life upon visit of estranged daughter from Australia. *Published by: Tinderbox Theatre Company. Tel: 01232 439313.*

1998	Second-Hand Thunder	Joseph Crilly	7

Blackmail, murder and intrigue in Mid-Ulster between 1976 and 1996. *Published by: Tinderbox Theatre Company. Tel: 01232 439313.*

ULSTER THEATRE COMPANY

Year	Title	Author	Cast Size
1994	Cinderella	Michael Poynor & Mark Dougherty	8

New commedia/burlesque pantomimic version.

1995	Jack and the Beanstalk	Michael Poynor & Mark Dougherty	12

New commedia/burlesque pantomimic version.

1996	Sleeping Beauty	Michael Poynor & Mark Dougherty	8

New commedia/burlesque pantomimic version.

1997	Scrooge's Christmas	Michael Poynor & Mark Dougherty	9

New commedia/burlesque pantomimic adaptation based on Dicken's 'A Christmas Carol'.

1998	Rockin' Mikado	Michael Poynor & Mark Dougherty	30

Set in modern Japan with local accents, an updated version of the G&S operetta.

UPSTATE THEATRE PROJECT

Year	Title	Author	Cast Size
1998	Hades	Declan Gorman	5

Partly devised with actors and youth groups: Intercutting scenes and dreams of a fictitious border community during a year of hope.

YEW THEATRE COMPANY

Year	Title	Author	Cast Size
1995	Chambers	Anne Barrett	2

A claustrophobic story of a provo-on-the-run and a failed dancer in whose apartment he is holed-up.

1996	A Moving Destiny	Deirdre Anne Hines	11

A journey through modern Ireland guided by three generations of a travelling family.

1997	Melting Doves	Max Hafler	5

Welcome to Club Soluble, where all your dreams dissolve! An elastic day and night in the West.

Appendix 2 New Irish Dance Works 1988-1998

COISCÉIM DANCE THEATRE

Year	Title	Choreographer	Cast	On Video
1995	Dances With Intent	David Bolger (co-choreography 'Taps with Sax' with Diane Richardson)	6	Yes

A combination of three dance pieces linked by the saxophone: "Taps With Sax", "Hon Nin Myo", and "Temporary Arrangements". Original music by Kenneth Edge.

Year	Title	Choreographer	Cast	On Video
1995	Reel Luck	David Bolger	5	Yes

A fast paced journey to present day Ireland, 'Reel Luck' captures the pace of transformation in Irish culture over recent decades. Original music by Kenneth Edge.

Year	Title	Choreographer	Cast	On Video
1995	Straight With Curves	David Bolger	3	Yes

A study of the moving body inspired by the works of Rodin. Original music by Kenneth Edge.

Year	Title	Choreographer	Cast	On Video
1996	Dragons And Tonics	Liz Roche	4	Yes

An illustration of ideas, 'Dragons And Tonics' plays with duality, internal conversations, physicality, fluidity and time. Original music by Denis Roche.

Year	Title	Choreographer	Cast	On Video
1997	Hit And Run	David Bolger	8	Yes

'Hit And Run' enters the twilight zone where power, corruption and violence are the forces that determine survival. Original music by Bell Helicopter.

Year	Title	Choreographer	Cast	On Video
1997	Back In Town	David Bolger	6	Yes

'Back In Town' explores with passion and vulnerability, the lyrical poetry of Phil Lynott's words from the music of Thin Lizzy.

Year	Title	Choreographer	Cast	On Video
1997	Ballads	David Bolger	6	Yes

'Ballads' sets out to explore defining emotional moments in the psyche of Irish people. Original music by Bell Helicopter.

Year	Title	Choreographer	Cast	On Video
1998	Toupees And Snare Drums	(Blueprint Script by Gina Moxley) David Bolger	13	Yes

Set in the mid sixties, the heyday of the Showband era, 'Toupees And Snare Drums' charts a disastrous night at Dizzy Duffy's Dancehall. Original music by Bell Helicopter.

Year	Title	Choreographer	Cast	On Video
1998	Seasons	Muirne Bloomer, Allan Irvine, Liz Roche	6	Yes

'Seasons' fuses choreographic styles to create a kaleidoscopic journey through Autumn, Winter, Spring and Summer. Original music by Bell Helicopter.

CORK CITY BALLET

Year	Title	Choreographer	Cast	On Video
1993	Persistence of Memory	Alan Foley	7	Yes

A ballet (featuring the classical talent of the company) with an original score by Cork Composer Colm O'Sullivan.

Year	Title	Choreographer	Cast	On Video
1994	Willing and Able	Alan Foley	10	Yes

A rock ballet with music by Prince, showing the range within the company.

Year	Title	Choreographer	Cast	On Video
1996	Celtic Dreams	Alan Foley	7	Yes

A neo-classical ballet fusing classical ballet with Irish dancing to the music of Irish artists.

DAGHDHA DANCE COMPANY

Year	Title	Choreographer	Cast	On Video
1990	Homing In	Mary Nunan	5	Yes

Piece for young audiences. The choreography was created around the activities of a not so ordinary family. Original music by Jules Maxwell.

Year	Title	Choreographer	Cast	On Video
1991	Heartscore	Mary Nunan	5	Yes

Piece for young audiences about young love and adolescent fears and hopes. Original music by Jules Maxwell.

Year	Title	Choreographer	Cast	On Video
1991	Through An Eye Of Stone	Mary Nunan	3	Yes

An abstract piece creating collaborations with a set and costume designer portraying a landscape of flowing water, fish and birds. Original music by Micheál Ó Súilleabháin.

Year	Title	Choreographer	Cast	On Video
1992	On Time With Pigs	Mary Nunan	4	Yes

For young audiences this piece portrays a sense of that timeless timekeeper - powerful, yet fragile in breath. Original music by Jules Maxwell.

Year	Title	Choreographer	Cast	On Video
1993	Territorial Claims	Mary Nunan	4	Yes

A comment on the battle for cultural identity featuring elements of the traditional Irish hornpipe. Original music by Tommy Hayes.

Year	Title	Choreographer	Cast	On Video
1993	For Company	Mary Nunan	5	Yes

Inspired by the novel 'Company' by Samuel Beckett. Choreography revolves around a lonely man who calls up memories of birth and death and the time between. Original music by Mike O'Mahoney.

Year	Title	Choreographer	Cast	On Video
1994	Like Writing on Water	Mary Nunan	3	Yes

Minimalist piece for 3 female dancers in which shapes emerge and dissolve with very small detailed gestures. Original music by Michael Seaver.

Year	Title	Choreographer	Cast	On Video
1995	This Way Up	Mary Nunan	4	Yes

For young audiences. Plays with shape using a ladder as a prop. Original music by Jules Maxwell.

Year	Title	Choreographer	Cast	On Video
1995	Fictional	Mary Nunan	5	Yes

A piece of physical theatre/dance portraying the inability of bureaucratic structures to fulfil the emotional needs of one individual. Original music by Michael Seaver.

Year	Title	Choreographer	Cast	On Video
1995	Useful Information for Potential Basketball Referees	Paul Johnson	4	Yes

For young audiences, the choreography develops and abstracts the gestures used by basketball referees. Original music by Michael Seaver .

Year	Title	Choreographer	Cast	On Video
1996	A World Apart	Paul Johnson	4	Yes

For young audiences, abstract work inspired by the Australian landscape. Original music by Michael Seaver

Year	Title	Choreographer	Cast	On Video
1996	Tales Of The Unexpected	Mary Nunan	4	Yes

For young audiences. A humorous piece based around the characters of Batman and Robin. Original music by Michael Seaver.

JOHN SCOTT'S IRISH MODERN DANCE THEATRE

Appendix 3 New Irish Operas 1988-1998

THE ARK, A CULTURAL CENTRE FOR CHILDREN

Year	Title	Libretto	Composer	Cast	Musicians
1998	The Pied Piper	Johnny Hanrahan	John Browne	11	4

An original 60 minute contemporary opera for children (7 - 13 years). 3 singers, 4 musicians and 8 children.

OPERA THEATRE COMPANY

Year	Title	Libretto	Composer	Cast	Musicians
1991	The Poet & His Double	Raymond Deane	Raymond Deane	5	6

23 minute chamber opera depicting imaginary meeting between Shelley and Artaud.

1991	The Words Upon The Windowpane	Hugh Maxton	John Buckley	5	6

20 minute chamber opera adaptation of Yeats' play.

1991	Hot Food With Strangers	Judy Kravis	Marian Ingoldsby	5	6

17 minute chamber opera set on a suburban railway, a dreamy depiction of desires.

1991	Position 7	James Conway	Kenneth Chalmers	1	5

15 minute solo opera dealing with a hostage's experience and memories.

1992	Sensational!	Gerard Stembridge	Kevin O'Connell	3	5

18 minute opera about scandal and gossip columns; to accompany Monteverdi's 'Orfeo'.

1992	Bitter Fruit	Nell McCafferty	Fergus Johnston	3	5

20 minute chamber opera presenting the conflict of a Bishop, a Judge and a mother for a child's life; to accompany Monteverdi's 'Orfeo'

1994	Frankie's	James Conway	Kenneth Chalmers	5	5

20 minute chamber opera describing events in a Scots-Italian chipper in 1939; commissioned to accompany 'I Pagliacci'.

1997	My Love, My Umbrella	James Conway	Kevin O'Connell	4	5

50 minute chamber opera adapted from three stories by John McGahern.

1998	The Wall of Cloud	Raymond Deane	Raymond Deane	4	7

Chamber opera in prologue and three acts loosely based on 8th Century Chinese play.